Forbidden City

Forbidden City

FRANCES WOOD

THE BRITISH MUSEUM PRESS

© 2005 The Trustees of The British Museum

First published in 2005 by The British Museum Press
A division of The British Museum Company Ltd
38 Russell Square, London WC1B 3QQ

Frances Wood has asserted the right to be identified as the author
of this work

A catalogue record for this book is available from the British Library

ISBN-13: 978-0-7141-2789-7

ISBN-10: 0-7141-2789-2

Designed and typeset in Galliard by Janet James

Printed and bound in China by C&C Offset Printing Co., Ltd

Contents

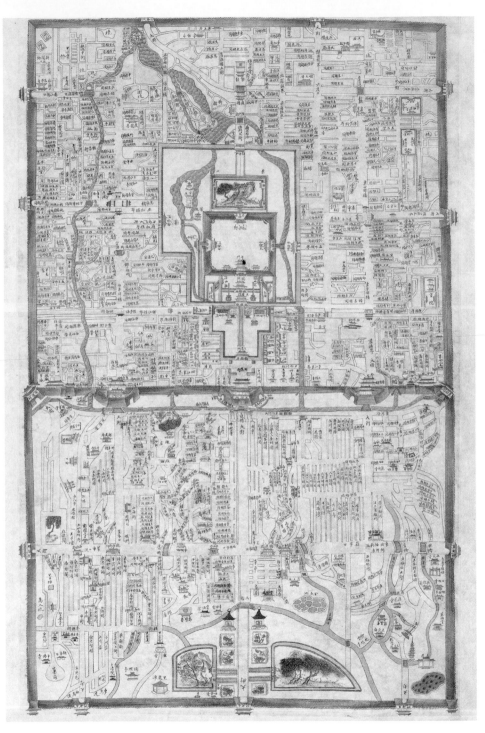

A manuscript map of Beijing
with the Forbidden City in the centre.
Based on a printed original, mid 19th century.

LEFT
Depictions of five-
clawed dragons were
supposed to be
restricted to imperial
use so this 15th-
century panel from a
cabinet may have come
from the Forbidden
City. Lacquer was
originally used as wood
protective, but during
the Ming deeply carved
multi-layered red
lacquer was popular
for bowls, boxes
and furniture.

RIGHT
Decorated with
peaches, a symbol of
longevity, this large
vase could have been
made for one of the
Qianlong emperor's
birthdays. The accurate
details of birds, leaves,
flowers and fruit were
achieved in overglaze
enamel colours,
painted onto plain
porcelain vessels
shipped north from
Jingdezhen.

The original 'cup-floating stream', where scholars drank and recited poetry together, was near Shaoxing in southern China. The Qianlong emperor was so taken with the idea that he had this stone channel constructed in a pavilion in the Forbidden City, and another in a temple outside the city where he liked to stay.

A Ming 'crown' of gilt silver filigree decorated with kingfisher wings and hard stones. It is a kinetic construction: the flimsy golden flower-heads, dragons and phoenixes dangle and would have swayed as the empress moved.

ABOVE
Jade, used since
Neolithic times, was a
highly prized material,
used for the finest
imperial goods in the
Forbidden City. Jade
books like this are
carved with
inscriptions in the
Qianlong emperor's
calligraphy and have
elaborately carved
covers, demonstrating
the emperor's skill
and intellect as well
as his wealth.

ABOVE
The Ming emperors stayed
within the Forbidden City
but the Manchus favoured
summer residences out in
the northern mountains
where they could hunt and
live out of doors like their
ancestors. Matteo Ripa, a
Jesuit at the court,
produced drawings of the
imperial retreat, 1714, and
the Qianlong emperor
wrote poems in its praise.

Introduction: Origins

Deep red, brilliant yellow and white, the Forbidden City, a massive seventy-two-hectare enclosure, is a block of colour at the centre of the grey Chinese capital, Beijing. For some five hundred years, it was successively occupied by twenty-four emperors and their vast retinue of servants, as well as housing the centre of government. It was set apart by its immense walls and gates, through its symbolism as the residence of heaven's representative on earth, and by those vibrant colours, forbidden by law to the ordinary residents of Beijing who lived in low grey houses. The sea of grey, high walls, washed a deep red, enclosed a series of long courtyards filled with buildings of all sizes set on white marble platforms and topped with roofs of brilliant yellow-glazed tiles.

To the Chinese observer, the yellow roofs visible above the surrounding walls immediately indicated the imperial presence for, in the Ming and Qing, yellow was the imperial colour (in the Han it had been black). The symbolism of yellow was associated with a series of linked concepts, which had their origins in yin and yang dualism and the Five Elements. The dialectical view of the cosmos, divided between yin (soft, dark, feminine, yielding) and yang (dominant, hard, bright and strong) first appears in the eighth century BC and was developed to include the Five Elements: water, fire, wood, metal and earth, from which 'all living things were created'[1] and incorporated into a system which included colour, direction and emotion.[2]

The name of the Forbidden City in Chinese is *Zi jin cheng*. *Zi* is a contraction of *ziwei*, or Pole Star. Fixed at the top of the heavenly vault with the subordinate stars arranged around it, the Pole Star was the residence of the supreme deity. The emperor of China was the 'son of heaven', the earthly equivalent of the supreme deity on the Pole Star. The second character means 'forbidden', and the Forbidden City was indeed inaccessible to ordinary people: only the highest officials or generals were allowed within its walls on official business. The last character, *cheng*, means wall or walled enclosure.

The Forbidden City was begun in 1406 and is the last of the great imperial palace compounds to have existed in China. It represents the culmination of several thousands of years of development of Chinese architectural techniques and ideas. It is also the last of many imperial palaces to have been built in Beijing.

Though there is evidence of human occupation from 500,000 years ago, Beijing gained in significance in the tenth century and became the site of a series of capital cities. The Khitan, a semi-nomadic people from northeast of Beijing, ruled the north of China from Beijing under the dynastic name of Liao from 947 to 1125.[3] The Liao dynasty was succeeded by the Jin, established in 1125 by the Jurchen, another tribe from the northeast,[4] whose way of life was more settled than that of the Khitan. Beijing served as their base for continuing assaults on the Song dynasty (960–1279).

In 1215, the Jin were driven out of Beijing by the invading Mongols who built a new capital and conquered the rest of China to rule as the Yuan dynasty from 1271 to 1368. The Yuan palace enclosure was locked up to save it from looting when the Mongols were overthrown by the Ming in 1368. In 1644, the Ming dynasty fell to the invading Manchus who ruled from the Forbidden City until 1911, when a Republic was declared. From 1406 until today, with a brief interlude from 1928 to 1949, Beijing has been the capital of China and was the seat of imperial power from 1406 to 1911 (though the deposed last emperor of the Qing, Puyi, lived on in the Forbidden City until 1924).

The history of royal and imperial palaces and their spatial and symbolic significance in China can be traced back to the earliest settlements where encircling walls, central palaces and the orientation of buildings towards the south became established features. The first secure evidence of 'capital' cities survives from the Shang (1600–1046 BC) when the political might of the city was 're-inforced with plans that put the leader in the very middle'.[5] An early depiction of the 'ruler's city' shows a square enclosure surrounded by high walls and soaring gates with a square enclosure at the very centre, the ruler's palace, the ancestor of the Forbidden City.[6]

That the emperor, heaven's representative on earth, was enthroned at the centre of a square enclosure was appropriate, for in traditional Chinese cosmology the earth was square. Heaven was circular, as can be seen in the form of the Halls of the Temple of Heaven, first built in 1420, at the same time as the Forbidden City (see plan, p. 6).

The gates, courtyards and halls of the Forbidden City rise through clouds, for the emperor was traditionally obscured from the view of ordinary people. In the foreground, officials in black ear-flapped hats bow as servants take their horses, for only the emperor could ride inside the palace. Painting attributed to Zhu Bang, 1500.

1

Building a palace

Today's Forbidden City is that of the Ming and Qing. Its construction relied upon improvements to the Grand Canal, enabling the movement of building materials and food to the capital. The first Ming emperor made Nanjing his capital, and the move to Beijing in the early fifteenth century was made by the Yongle emperor. His father had chosen his eldest son as his heir in accordance with the Chinese system of primogeniture, and sent many of his other sons out to rule different parts of the empire, to control the borders and prevent jealousy within the palace. His fourth son, the future Yongle emperor, was enfeoffed in Beijing and, after seizing power from his nephew and destroying much of Nanjing, decided to remove the capital to his old territory.

There was opposition to the move, for some believed the fall of the Mongol Yuan dynasty with its capital at the very same place had 'exhausted its fortunes', but this was countered with the view of Zhu Xi (1130–1200), one of the greatest Confucian philosophers, that Beijing had 'superior' fengshui.[7]

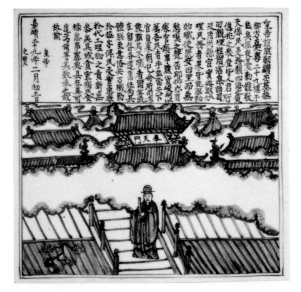

Underglaze blue tile dated 1551, showing an official holding his ivory tally and standing in front of palatial buildings concealed by clouds. The text is an imperial edict reminding officials to govern competently and warning of punishment for misbehaviour.

Preserved from harm during the fighting, the Yuan imperial palace was finally demolished to make way for Yongle's Forbidden City, but the lakes dug out by the Jin (1115–1234) for their imperial garden were retained and their water supply improved to provide for further ponds within the palace enclosure. The construction of the Forbidden City, the 'palace city' of 9,000 rooms, took place between 1417 and 1420, and most of it was designed by a eunuch called Nguyen An from Annam who died in 1453.[8] Within the main enclosure were more enclosures: a series of courtyards arranged on regular axes, running south to north, their main halls facing south.

The three main halls of the southern part of the Forbidden City, roofed with yellow-glazed tiles, their facades painted dull red, stand on white marble platforms above huge courtyards paved with specially made grey bricks. Here officials waited before dawn to see the emperor.

Another planning principle was the placing of more public areas to the front (south) of the enclosure and the private dwelling areas to the rear. In the Forbidden City, inside the towering Meridian Gate and raised high on a great marble platform, were three major halls used for official business. Behind them, in the inner (residential) palace, were a further three halls, set lower and surrounded by smaller courtyards in which the imperial family and servants lived. Imperial audiences and receptions for government ministers, generals, high officials and foreign envoys were held in the outer court but the inner palace was closed to all but the imperial family and their servants and eunuchs.

Before construction could begin, the materials necessary to construct '9,000 rooms' had to be brought to Beijing. In August 1406, Yongle sent envoys all over China to collect timber and stone and to supervise the production of bricks and tiles. Timber supplies included elm, oak, camphor, catalpa and fir from the provinces of Zhejiang, Jiangxi, Hunan and Hubei, but the most impressive were the huge trunks of the nanmu (*Phoebe nanmu*), a durable, close-grained hardwood that grew in Sichuan, some 1,500 kilometres southwest of Beijing. Almost all Chinese buildings were constructed with a wooden framework of upright pillars that carried the roof; in lesser structures, smaller tree-trunks or even composite columns made of different bits of wood would suffice, but for the Forbidden City hundreds of thousands of massive, solid trunks of nanmu were required. The logs were shipped from the Sichuan mountains in the rainy season, floated down smaller rivers until they reached the Yangtze and then pulled along the Grand Canal. It took three or four years for each log to reach Beijing. Even after the main phase of construction was over, the supply was maintained so that new buildings could be constructed or repairs carried out, and it was estimated that in 1437 there were more than 380,000 pieces of timber stored in the imperial timberyard.[9]

Though timber was the main structural material, imperial palaces also required a considerable amount of fine stone to raise platforms on which to build the halls and gates. It is generally true that the grander a Chinese building, the higher it is raised above ground level, and that principle can be seen clearly in the Forbidden City where the imperial halls, in which the emperor sat and conducted state affairs, are raised on massive triple platforms of white marble whilst the domestic buildings to the rear are only slightly raised above ground level.

The finest marble was quarried at Fangshan some fifty kilometres west of Beijing. There were two main types: a hard white marble with a slight green tinge, known as 'mugwort marble', which was used for the huge dragon-carved slabs over which the emperor was carried into the halls in his sedan chair, and 'white jade' marble which was used for the carved balustrades surrounding all the terraces and bridges of the Forbidden City. The size, especially of the mugwort marble slabs, was enormous. On the terraces, slabs at least seven metres long were required to fill the space between the nanmu cedar columns, and the carved slabs over which the emperor was carried could weigh as much as 5,000 kilogrammes. An account survives of the transportation of the slab to be placed in front of the Hall of Supreme Harmony when it was rebuilt in the reign of the Wanli emperor of the Ming (1573–1620). The piece of marble was more than ten metres long and weighed about 180 tons. The only way to move it was in winter. Wells were dug at intervals of one *li* (a Chinese mile, about half a kilometre) along the route and water was thrown over the road to provide a slippery, iced surface over which the vast slab was dragged. It took over 20,000 workers more than twenty-eight days to move the stone to Beijing.

The labourers who transported the marble, and others who worked to construct the Forbidden City, were directed by the Minister of Works, Wu Zhong (1372–1442). Much labour was contributed by ordinary Chinese as part of the service owed to the emperor as a form of taxation. Walls, roads, irrigation works and palace buildings had for millennia been built by men conscripted as part of the tax system, but Wu Zhong was also Minister of Justice and, on his orders, the labour force was greatly increased by prisoners serving their sentences on the imperial building sites.[10] Some of these must have worked in some discomfort since they were expected to continue to wear the cangue, a heavy wooden board with a hole at the centre (like a portable version of the stocks), although hand-cuffs were removed on site.[11]

Many of the other building materials for the Forbidden City were found or made in distant parts of the country. Though much lime was quarried near Zhoukoudian and in the counties surrounding Beijing, other sources of high quality lime were in Shanxi and Jiangxi provinces. Red clay to wash the walls and fix roof tiles was extracted and processed in Shandong province, yellow clay from Hebei was used to colour the walls of the great halls, and fine gold leaf, used in much architectural decoration, on red dragon pillars, gable decorations and elsewhere, came from Suzhou.[12]

Many other prisoners and forced labourers worked to produce bricks and tiles. Many types of brick were used in the construction of the Forbidden City. The great courtyards are paved with 'settled clay bricks' from Linqing in Shandong, which were fine-grained and able to withstand wear as a surface paving. Linqing was on the Grand Canal and local transportation regulations were altered to stipulate that all barges carrying grain past Linqing had to carry a load of 'settled clay bricks' to Beijing. External corridors and interiors were paved with dark grey 'metal bricks' in varying sizes. The name derived from the ringing sound they made when struck. These were made in the Suzhou and Songjiang areas and shipped up the Grand Canal.

The great variety of tiles required were produced in Beijing. The majority of the roof tiles were yellow-glazed. Some of the smaller buildings had plain grey-tiled roofs. One of the tile-works was to the southeast of the city, now occupied by the Taoranting park whose lakes were formed by the extraction of clay for tile-making. Another tile-works was in the present-day Liulichang area, southwest of the Forbidden City, for hundreds of years the centre of the antique and anti-quarian book trade in Beijing. The name of the main street, Liulichang, means 'glazed tile works', reflecting its earlier status. Later in the Ming, an imperial edict ordered that ceramic production be moved outside the city for fear of pollution from the gases released during firing and because of the threat of fire itself.[13]

Apart from plain and glazed roof-tiles, in flat or cylindrical form, an extraordinary range of decorative tiles was also used. Their forms and decoration often reflected Chinese beliefs about the special vulnerability of the eaves of a building to evil spirits and the general susceptibility of timber-framed buildings to fire, which could be combated by reference to various sorts of

A series of ceramic animals are set along the eaves. They include protective lions and mythical beasts, with a horned dragon, associated with fire-preventing water, at the rear. In front, the man riding on a chicken is said to be Prince Min of Qi, hanged as a traitor from the eaves of his palace and here serving as a warning to others.

dragons. In contrast to Western fire-breathing dragons, dragons in China were associated with water: they either lived in rivers or in the rain-bearing clouds, and they had the power to attract and control water. They were also, if five-clawed, one of the most common symbols for the emperor himself. All the eaves on all of the buildings in the Forbidden City had circular end tiles and triangular drainage tiles, impressed with a variety of designs (most often the imperial dragon or auspicious characters).

The forms of the roofs varied greatly. Pavilions with conical roofs, like the Pavilion of One Thousand Autumns, and halls with hipped pavilion roofs, like the Hall of Complete Harmony, were topped with giant yellow-glazed bosses. On other halls, built-up ridges of glazed tile work ran across the top of the roof and often down to the eaves. At either end of the main horizontal ridge are *chiwen* dragons (particularly water-loving dragons), their bodies bent backwards and gaping jaws engulfing the end of the ridge. Lines of fierce animal figures are often placed on the ridge that runs down towards the eaves. They include lions (protectors, derived from the protective lions of Buddhism), dragons and phoenixes, symbolizing the emperor and empress, sea-horses that gambol in fire-extinguishing water, and a figure riding a chicken, thought to represent the legendary tyrant Prince Min of Qi who was hanged from the eaves as a lesson to others. All these ceramic figures, varying in size according to the size of the roof, were moulded, glazed and fired to specification. And, since accidental damage or gradual weathering affected the buildings in the Forbidden City, the roofs with all their different end-tiles and ceramic figures were frequently renewed, requiring further firings.

Under the supervision of Nguyen An, one million convict and conscript labourers did the heavy work on site whilst 100,000 specialized craftsmen worked on timber construction, decorative lattice-work and stone-carving. The master mason was Lu Xiang, who had learnt his craft from his father and had worked on the first Ming palace in Nanjing. It is said the thousand dragon-head drainage spouts on the marble platform supporting the Hall of Supreme Harmony are his work. Like Lu Xiang, the master carpenter, Kuai Xiang, came from a family of carpenters in Suzhou and had also worked on the Nanjing palace before moving to Beijing to work on the Forbidden City.

After the master carpenters had erected the timber-frame halls and master tilers had laid the shiny black floor tiles, all the exterior and many of the interior timbers were painted. The exterior columns of nanmu cedar were protected against the elements with a coating made of hemp, clay, pig's blood and tong oil, then painted crimson. The crossbeams beneath the yellow-tiled eaves, and the timber brackets supporting the eaves were painted with polychrome decorations – often with the imperial symbol of the dragon inside geometric cartouches – and the ends of the rafters were decorated with the Buddhist swastika, an emblem of good fortune, or auspicious characters such as that meaning longevity. The timber interiors of the main halls were similarly decorated and sometimes the main columns were gilded and decorated with low-relief dragons. The interior timbers of the more domestic buildings were sometimes left plain, simply polished with tong oil or decorated in a softer style with flower and landscape paintings in cartouches outlined with scrolling and curlicues.[14]

Within three years, between 1417 and 1420, the Forbidden City was finished. Its red-washed walls encircled an area 961 metres long and 753 metres wide. Outside was the imperial city, protected by a 52-metre wide moat and a 10-metre high wall. Within the Forbidden City, entered by the towering Meridian

Gate, were six main yellow-tiled halls raised on white marble platforms on the central axis and, to the rear, many lower yellow-roofed halls. Here the imperial family and its retinue of maids and eunuchs moved in at the beginning of 1421 to live amongst libraries, studies, temples and gardens. The palace fitted to perfection the stipulation of the *Li Ji* or *Book of Rites* (traditionally ascribed to Confucius) that 'court affairs should be to the front, sleeping quarters to the rear'. Even its sleeping arrangements echoed the beliefs in yin-yang and the Five Elements that governed so much imperial symbolism. The empress and concubines lived on the west side of the inner court, associated with the fruitfulness of autumn, whilst the emperor and his sons lived on the east, governed by the element of wood and the vitality of spring.

Only a hundred days after it was officially occupied, the three major halls, the Respect Heaven Hall, Flower-covered Hall and Prudence Hall (later reconstructed and renamed the Hall of Supreme Harmony, Hall of Complete Harmony and Hall of Preserving Harmony), were all burned down, possibly following a lightning strike. The emperor's critics seized upon this disaster as a sign that heaven was angry with Yongle. It gave new impetus to those who felt that the capital should have remained in Nanjing. Yongle did not return to

Long corridors separate the different dwellings in the rear part of the palace. This area was comparatively empty during the Ming, but filled up during the Qing when it was customary for sons to stay within the family home. Eunuchs lit lanterns before dawn and again in the evening.

Nanjing but continued to hold court in the Gate of Serving Heaven, which had survived the conflagration.

The Yongle emperor died in Mongolia in 1424 and was the first emperor to be buried in the hills northwest of Beijing, in the Ming tombs enclosure. It was not until 1439, during the reign of the sixth Ming emperor, that the decision was made to reconstruct the three main halls, under the direction of the Minister of Works, Wu Zhong, who had been in charge of the original construction.

Over the next 450 years, the capital was securely established in Beijing and the Forbidden City was the home of the emperors. It was not, however, unchanged, for the expansion in size of the court and the susceptibility to fire of the timber-framed halls meant much new building. A chronology of the Forbidden City lists an unending series of new constructions, disastrous fires and reconstructions. In 1449, the Hall of Literary Profundity, which housed the entire imperial library, burned down. In 1514, the New Year firework display set fire to the Palace of Heavenly Purity and the Palace of Earthly Tranquillity, and, in 1531, the corner tower of the Meridian Gate was struck by lightning.

In 1535 the names of twelve palaces were changed, many to be changed again in 1562. Thus the Hall of Eternal Happiness was renamed the Hall of Nourishing Virtue in 1535 and then the Hall of Eternal Longevity, and the Hall of Eternal Spring became the Hall of Eternal Tranquillity and then reverted to the Hall of Eternal Spring in the late Ming. It is clear that the names were intended to bring longevity, tranquillity, virtue and happiness to their occupants, and changes sometimes reflected a change in the use of the building or a deliberate attempt to refresh the 'good luck' of the site after a disaster.

When the Manchu Qing dynasty took control of China in 1644, one of the first things to happen to the Forbidden City was the renaming of the three main halls with the titles they still bear: Supreme Harmony, Complete Harmony and Preserving Harmony. This was followed by fifty years of renovation and reconstruction. The Qianlong emperor, who reigned from 1736 to 1795, was an incredible builder. Before he ascended the throne, he had ignored the Ming Chinese belief (which went back to the time of Confucius) that the emperor and his sons should live on the eastern side of the Inner Court, moving his residence to the Palace of Double Glory on the west. This may have been because, as a Manchu, he could ignore aspects of Chinese superstition.[15]

When he was emperor, Qianlong ordered the construction of 360 rooms to house the royal princes, who, in a break with Ming practice, all stayed in the Forbidden City. The Manchus did not follow primogeniture; instead they chose the best-suited prince as heir, keeping his name secret until his accession. The princes' twenty-seven classrooms were renovated and Qianlong also oversaw the construction of the Palace of Tranquil Longevity to the east of the Inner Palace where he intended to retire. After his major additions to the Forbidden City, fires and rebuildings continued throughout the Qing.[16]

2

Officials and eunuchs

S hut away in the Forbidden City, the emperor was ultimately responsible for the affairs of the country over which he ruled, according to Chinese belief, with the mandate of heaven. If all was well, the harvests were good, the flood defences on the major rivers kept up and the people's livelihood ensured, then heaven would be happy. The imperial response to natural disasters like drought and floods was significant but, sheltered from the outside world in the Forbidden City, the emperor relied upon his local officials to inform him and to act according to local conditions and local needs.

The Yongle emperor presided over an audience at dawn, when high officials, each holding an oblong ivory tally issued by the eunuchs of the Seal Office which indicated that they were allowed into the Forbidden City, stood below him. At noon there was another audience, attended by senior officials and ministers. But most government involved paperwork, in the form of local government reports known as memorials. More than a hundred memorials poured in every day, from all corners of the country, to the Office of Transmission. They were sorted by eunuchs and passed to the Directorate of Ceremonial and sent to the emperor for

Officials approach the Meridian gate, one prostrating himself on the central path, reserved for the emperor. Only officials of the highest rank were allowed inside the Forbidden City for imperial audiences. An illustration from the memoirs of a Manchu official, Linqing (1791–1846), published 1847–50.

consideration. He marked them in red (only the emperor could use red ink) and sent them back for redrafting. In the evening, the emperor went through them all again and, when he was satisfied and had signed them off in red ink, they were returned through the Directorate of Ceremonial to the Office of Transmission for dispatch throughout the country.

The emperor stood at the pinnacle of a vast bureaucracy and only the most significant memorials made it all the way to the Forbidden City. The vast bureaucracy first established in the Han dynasty (206 BC–AD 221) was composed of centrally appointed officials, selected on the basis of examinations. During the Ming, around 22,000 local officials ruled over the fifteen provinces, serving as district magistrates, responsible to the sub-prefect and prefect with an administrative commissioner at the provincial level. One of the most important tasks for the district officials was the collection of tax to support the government, based upon registration of households and land. There were two annual collections of agricultural tax, the summer tax (winter wheat and other early crops) and the autumn tax, collected mainly in rice. Tax could also be paid in the form of rolls of silk, and households were expected to take part in labour service, or pay someone else to do it.

The officials were selected through an examination system, restored by the first Ming emperor in 1384. He also set up a system of free government schools to prepare boys for the official examinations. Every three years, two sessions of preliminary exams were held in prefectural cities and successful graduates were known as *xiucai*, or 'flowering talents'. *Xiucai* were exempt from the labour service and certain punishments and were held in great local esteem. To progress, however, a *xiucai* needed to go to the provincial capital to take the exam that would make him a *juren*, 'recommended man', eligible to take a further exam in Beijing. Exams in the provincial capitals and in Beijing were taken in specially constructed compounds with hundreds of little cells where candidates were literally locked in with food and water for several days. Success in the Beijing exam meant that the *jinshi* or 'presented scholar' was summoned to the Hall of Preserving Harmony in the Forbidden City for a further test presided over by the emperor; only after that would he be offered an official rank and a post in the government.[17]

Though in theory open to all, the cost of education and the time it took to pass the necessary series of official exams meant that the poor could not really hope to enter the bureaucracy. The exam syllabus was entirely based on memorizing the ancient Confucian Classics and approved commentaries. The Yongle emperor ordered officially sanctioned publications of the *Four Books* and *Five Classics* in 1417, so unorthodox commentary was excluded and students knew exactly what they were meant to think.[18] The often abstruse ideas expressed in these very ancient texts gave rise to

A 19th-century portrait of the Yongle emperor of the Ming, who was born in 1360, and ruled from 1402 to 1424. He ordered the construction of the Forbidden City when he moved the capital from Nanjing to Beijing. Though crude, the portrait shows him in Ming costume with a low round-necked gown.

examination questions in which future district magistrates and tax collectors were asked to discuss phrases like 'Where the people rest' from the *Great Learning* or 'Scrupulous in his own conduct and lenient only in his dealings with the people' from the *Confucian Analects*.[19] Moreover, from 1487, answers were required in a set form, which became known as the 'eight-legged essay', of no longer than 700 characters arranged under eight main headings.

The government officials who reported directly to the emperor in the Forbidden City were his three Grand Secretaries and his six Ministers of Personnel, Rites, War, Public Works, Revenue, and Punishment. Also reporting directly were the five Chief Military Commissioners and the Board of Censors, which sent out upright young officials to monitor the conduct of local government, the contents of the state granaries and the administration of justice.

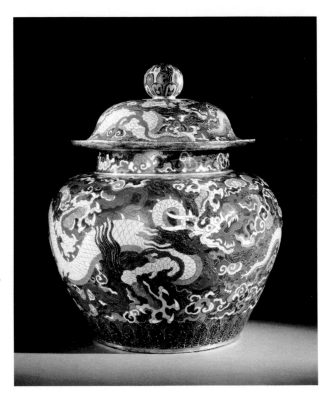

Large cloisonné jar with lid and with the mark of the Xuande reign period (1426–35). Such five clawed dragons were supposed to be restricted to imperial wares. Ceramics and bronzes of the Xuande period are considered particularly fine and the emperor himself enjoyed painting. Early 15th century.

In many ways, the effectiveness of the government depended upon the attitude of the emperor. Yongle felt it important that he see every memorial, but towards the end of the Ming the picture was very different. Yongle's son, who ruled only for one year (1424–5), was also personally involved, contradicting the Minister of Revenue over famine relief and the Ministries of Revenue and Works on tax remission in stricken areas.[20]

The Xuande emperor (r. 1426–35) had good relations with his Grand Secretaries, bringing bottles of fine wine to discussions. He and his successor were lucky in that the three Grand Secretaries were good officials with a long record of service in the imperial household. Xuande's eldest son never missed the daily audiences, and the Hongzhi emperor (r. 1488–1505) was reported as rarely being late for the pre-dawn audience.[21] However, the Zhengde emperor (1506–21) refused to take part in audiences, the Jiajing emperor (1522–67) was not interested, and the Wanli emperor (1567–1620) fought with his Grand Secretaries and, towards the end of his reign, only saw them once in three years. From 1598 he refused to appear at the daily audiences and from 1591 refused to take part in the essential rituals. At the end of his reign, the country was in serious trouble, with prisoners dying in jail because there was no-one to try them and vacancies at the top of most of the ministries, whilst the emperor relied upon eunuchs to extract the enormous sums he required from the treasury to rebuild parts of the Forbidden City after fires in 1596 and 1597.

Throughout the Ming dynasty, the Forbidden City filled steadily with eunuchs. Eunuchs had been used from the Han dynasty as servants within the imperial palace because they were safe in the presence of women and could not interfere with the succession. Eunuch power grew in the Ming with the separation of living quarters (the inner court) and halls in which government business was conducted (the outer court). Apart from the emperor, eunuchs were the only people who could pass between the two. Many emperors regarded eunuchs as reliable, their loyalty vested in the imperial household rather than the outer world of government and politics and, when emperors such as those of the late Ming refused to see their officials, eunuchs became powerful go-betweens.

The eunuch Zheng He (1371–1433), who led seven great maritime expeditions to Africa and India, was a Muslim from the Yunnan province whose family had loyally served the Mongols under the Yuan dynasty. When he was eleven, Yunnan province fell to the Ming and his father was killed. The young Zheng He was taken to Nanjing as a prisoner of war and castrated. As a young castrated captive, he was given to the Yongle emperor and followed him to Beijing.

A detailed account of the method of voluntary castration survives from the 1870s. Prospective eunuchs, supported by guarantors, paid government-approved specialists to carry out the operation. The patient's stomach and upper thighs were tightly bound with bandages and the parts were washed three times in 'hot pepper-water'. He was held firmly by the surgeon's assistants and if he responded appropriately to the question, 'are you going to regret this?' the surgeon removed penis and scrotum with a small curved knife. A plug, or hot solder, was put into the urethra and the wound covered in paper soaked in cold water and bandaged up. The victim was then made to walk about for several hours. He was not allowed to drink for three days and then the plug was removed. If urine poured out of the wound, the operation had been successful. If it didn't, death was inevitable. After a hundred days, his wound healed, the new eunuch could apply to enter the imperial household. His 'treasure' (his severed genitals) was sealed in a special jar and kept on a high shelf, symbolizing the high office he hoped to obtain. It was important to keep his 'treasure' safe because he would have to present it as evidence to the head eunuch. Sometimes eunuchs lost their 'treasure', in which case they might buy, borrow or even rent another 'treasure'.[22]

To the Chinese, castration was a particularly severe punishment, for they believed that one's body, given by one's parents, should be carefully maintained as a matter of filial respect. Proper burial of the intact body was necessary to calm the soul, for if the body was not complete when buried, the anguished soul would wander eternally, trying to gather the separated parts. The 'treasure' had to be buried with its owner to prevent his soul wandering unhappily.

Eunuchs were said to walk with a mincing gait, were even more beardless than other Chinese, and had high voices. A side effect of the operation was urinary incontinence so they often smelt. Eunuchs were very sensitive about allusions to their condition, disliking the word for 'cut' and extending their sensitivity to the point where it was impolite to talk of bob-tailed dogs or teapots with broken handles in their presence.[23]

The first Ming emperor, Zhu Yuanzhang, was suspicious of officials, considering them neglectful, corrupt and hard-hearted.[24] He was not much keener on eunuchs: 'Not one or two of these people out of thousands are good . . . These people can only be given sprinkling and sweeping jobs. They should not be given responsibility and their number should not be large.'[25] During his reign, the number of eunuchs in the inner palace was no more than 400 and he ordered that they should not learn to read and write nor interfere with government affairs. He also prohibited castration except in the case of prisoners. Nevertheless, increasingly suspicious of his officials, he made considerable use of eunuchs as spies and, despite his strictures, there were 10,000 eunuchs in the palace by the end of the fifteenth century and 70,000 in 1644. These huge numbers were not the result of the castration of prisoners but an increase in the number of men who underwent voluntary castration in search of work in the Forbidden City.

Eunuchs became a complex commodity in the Ming. Like his father, the Yongle emperor employed eunuchs because he thought officials could be untrustworthy. In order to maintain the loyalty of his relatives, he offered them frequent gifts of silks, silver, gold and eunuchs. In the later reign of the Jingtai emperor (1450–57), the combination of an excess of self-castrated eunuchs seeking work and the obligation to send eunuchs as wedding presents to his many cousins led to his ordering a stockpile of eunuchs as future gifts to be kept under the control of the (eunuch-run) Directorate of Ceremonial.[26]

By 1453, eunuchs had become essential to the smooth running of the Forbidden City, let alone government. Within the Imperial City, surrounding the Forbidden City, there were at least twenty-four eunuch agencies serving the imperial household. The most important was the Directorate of Ceremonial which grew in importance through the Ming as it controlled the flow of government documents to and from the emperor, sorting and selecting items for imperial attention and giving advice on petitions. The three Grand Secretaries, civil officials and not eunuchs, were not allowed the same control and were not allowed into the Inner Court. The Directorate of Ceremonial was also in charge of all palace ceremonies, rituals and eunuch affairs, effectively running the Forbidden City.

The imperial archives, from Linqing's memoir, 'Tracks of a wild swan in the snow', 1847–50. During the Qing, the imperial archives were housed in a building to the east of the Forbidden City, set aside and constructed entirely from brick and tile, to protect the archives from the fires that frequently swept through the palace.

21

The Department of Palace Servants and the Department of Carpentry carried out all building work. The Palace Servants ran a team of artisans who worked inside the palace on a three-shift basis, on brickwork, stonework and painting, and on imperial building work outside the Forbidden City such as the construction of imperial tombs in the mausoleum north of Beijing and mansions for princes old enough to leave the palace. It supervised workshops and sources of supply such as the stone quarries near Hangzhou and timber forests all over the country. The Department of Carpentry organized the production of the highest quality screens, latticework windows and doors, fine furniture of bamboo and hardwood, lanterns, combs, buckets and decorative items like toys and artificial flowers.

The Outfitting Directorate supervised the production of soft furnishings: cushions for the hardwood chairs, blankets, sheets and towels as well as producing all the cloth items required for ceremony like umbrellas, tents and canopies and seasonal articles of clothing like rainwear. A separate Department of Imperial Clothing included tailors, hatters and shoemakers to provide all the immensely elaborate clothing needed by the imperial family and palace servants.

The Imperial Stables due east of Coal Hill housed the imperial horses, fed daily on black or yellow beans and straw (although they were allowed out to pasture in the summer and autumn) and also the elephants that pulled the imperial carriage to the Temple of Heaven, the emperor's cats, and exotic animals brought from abroad like the giraffes collected by the eunuch admiral Zheng He.

Between the Altar of Earth and Grain and the Spirit Terrace where eunuchs used astronomical instruments to observe the heavens, make predictions and advise the emperor on omens, was the Department of Toilet Paper where eunuchs manufactured the millions of sheets required annually. The emperor had special soft toilet paper made from different materials, but the standard paper was about two feet wide and made from straw, wood, oil and lime, stamped with a red mark and distributed where necessary in the Forbidden City. Baths were administered separately, with the Department of the Bathhouse supplying baths, bowls and bathwater as well as soap and washing materials. The Fire and Water Department supplied firewood for cooking, charcoal for braziers in the winter and oil for lamps and sacrifices. It was also responsible for filling the massive bronze vessels of water to help put out the fires common to the firework displays at New Year. The Fire and Water Department organized the annual cleaning of the moat around the Forbidden City every spring and removed imperial rubbish from the back gate on the fourth, fourteenth and twenty-fourth days of every month. Cleaning and sweeping was done by low-paid eunuchs.

The Palace Food Directorate and the Imperial Kitchen supplied many of the raw materials for the imperial table and processed them, using 10,000,000 kilos of rice, 100,000 jars of wine and seventy tons of salt a year preparing meals for up to 15,000 people every single day.[27] They also provided the raw material for sacrifices and the cooked food for offerings to the dead. Animals required for sacrifice had to be perfect, of the appropriate colour, with no markings on their

18th-century silver chafing dishes were specially made to keep the imperial food warm and safe as silver was supposed to indicate the presence of poison. Apart from special celebrations, the emperors and empresses might eat anywhere in the palace, perhaps at some distance from kitchens.

coats or skin and specially fed and fattened in the palace or temple grounds before being slaughtered. A hundred eunuchs ran farms that supplied mutton, geese, chickens and ducks. Eunuchs also ran the Imperial Wine Bureau which oversaw not only the production of wine but also the fermentation of soya beans for soya sauce and other soy products like bean curd and soya flour; they ran the imperial flour mill and the imperial vinegar works and the Bureau of Vegetable Gardening.[28] Up the Grand Canal came refrigerated barges carrying

'fresh plums, loquats, the fruit of the strawberry tree, fresh bamboo shoots and shad' and 'fresh tea, cassia, pomegranates, persimmons and tangerines . . . swans, vegetables . . . cherries preserved in honey . . . cormorants . . . water chestnuts, taro, ginger, lotus root . . . fragrant rice'.[29]

An 18th-century 'famille rose' enamelled vase of the Qianlong period with decoration of birds amongst flowers and fruit.

Meals for the emperor were served on gold dishes or specially ordered porcelains made in Jingdezhen in Jiangxi province and shipped smoothly up the Grand Canal. These were ordered in annual shipments of 10,000 pieces by the Directorate of Ceremonial. The emperor's meals were made by cooks from the Directory of Ceremonials during odd months, alternating with cooks from the Directorate of the Eastern Depot which was otherwise known and feared as a sort of eunuch secret police headquarters.[30] Eunuchs were also responsible for the Imperial Pharmacy (which used many medicinal items produced on the imperial farms), and for the storage of silver money collected as tax and luxury items, 'gold, silver, jewels, satin silks, high-quality wool fabric, jade, ivory, pearls, gems'[31] in the Imperial Treasury.

Eunuchs in the Inner Court Supplies Depot maintained a store of candles and incense and kept lamps burning all night in all the streets of the Forbidden City, whilst those from the Keys Storehouse locked all the gates and halls at dusk and opened them up again at 3 a.m. Eunuchs also kept the time in the Forbidden City. Ten worked all night watching the clepsydra or water clock and, as the water level indicated that an hour had passed, they ceremonially changed the 'hour tablets' in the Palace of Heavenly Purity. Throughout the night eunuchs from the Night Drum Room climbed the Xuanwu Gate at the back of the Forbidden City, beating a drum to indicate the five divisions of the night and ringing a bronze bell in between. Thus, during the Ming, eunuchs ran the entire imperial household as well as gradually taking control of all official communication with the emperor.

When the Manchus swept into China in 1644, overthrowing the Ming dynasty and establishing the Qing dynasty in its place, the position of the eunuchs changed. The Manchus were conscious that eunuch power had grown too strong in the late Ming and the collapse of the dynasty was partly ascribed to the weakness of the later emperors in allowing the eunuchs to accrue such power. The number of eunuchs was reduced to about 3,000, and a new group of palace servants was introduced, the Manchu bondservants, 'hereditarily servile people'.[32] They were not necessarily Manchu; indeed many were Chinese or other northeastern peoples taken captive during the period of the Manchu expansion and conquest from the beginning of the seventeenth century, and allocated to different 'banners'. The Banner system was established in 1601, dividing the Manchu soldiery into fighting groups under red, yellow, blue and white flags (with later subdivisions of 'bordered' banners with flags bordered with white or red). The inention was to break down earlier tribal divisions and eventually the entire Manchu population was divided into seven 'banners'.

The administration of the imperial household was eventually taken from the numerous eunuch directorates of the Ming and placed in the hands of the Neiwufu, the department of 'internal matters', which was staffed by bannermen. Like the proliferating departments of the Ming eunuchs, the Neiwufu covered an extraordinary range of activities, so that by the end of the nineteenth century it managed fifty-six sub-agencies: publishing fine-printed editions from the Wuyingdian or Hall of Military Eminence to the southwest of the Outer Court, running the monopoly on jade and ginseng, licensing the import of copper for coins, running pawnshops and workshops all over China as well as within the Forbidden City, and managing the stores, catering, entertainments, rituals, building, security and staffing of the imperial household.[33]

As at the end of the Ming, the imperial household became immensely corrupt and wasteful: the last emperor's tutor, Reginald Johnston, thought the Neiwufu was the 'vampire draining the life-blood of the dynasty'.[34] He suggested its growth was unchecked because no one ever sat down to do the sums, as 'mere money matters' were 'beneath the notice of a scholar and a gentleman.'[35]

Reginald Johnston was probably the last foreigner to work in the Forbidden

City, as one of the tutors of the last emperor from 1919 to 1922, but foreign envoys had visited it from the very beginning. The installation of the Yongle emperor in his new palace on New Year's day, 1421, was recorded by Hafiz-i Abru, an envoy sent by Shahrukh, Prince of Herat. He noted that all participants in the celebration were forbidden to wear anything white, because white is the Chinese colour of mourning. He was summoned at midnight and led through brightly-lit streets to the Forbidden City and installed with the other foreign envoys (from Southeast Asian countries, Korea, Japan, various parts of Central Asia and China's northern border neighbours) in one of the blue temporary tents that had been set up in the stone-flagged courtyard below the main hall. 'An army of 200,000 soldiers were guarding the area . . . there were about 2,000 people, with shield-sized Chinese fans of different shapes and colours on each one's shoulder. Some adult and child actors were performing.' He noted that 'access to the Inner Palace was forbidden' and described the celebration banquet. 'When the emperor was seated, all the envoys lined up before the throne and kowtowed [kneeling and touching their foreheads to the ground] five times. Then the emperor bade them sit at their tables on which servants place mutton, goose, chicken, rice wine and other types of food and drink. In the meantime, acrobatic performances took place.' Having started in the early hours of the morning at one of the coldest times of year, 'the celebration did not finish until a ceremony was held at noon. Then the emperor rewarded the actors and rose to go to the Inner Palace.'[36]

The first Westerner to enter the Forbidden City was not a diplomatic envoy but Matteo Ricci (1552–1610), a Jesuit missionary. Having studied Chinese in Macau in 1583, he and fellow-Jesuit Michèle Ruggieri became the first foreign missionaries to be allowed to live in China. Adopting the dress of a Chinese scholar, Ricci soon accommodated himself to the fact that Christianity on its own was not making much impression on the Chinese, and decided that he might do better by trying to infiltrate the highest echelons of society as a scientific specialist before, he hoped, resuming his missionary activities. Thus it was 'following his example that the seventeenth and eighteenth century Jesuits of China turned themselves into mathematicians, geographers, astronomers, doctors, painters and musicians' and more.[37]

Ricci made contact with members of the imperial family and high officials in Nanjing and first went to Beijing in 1598, but he found the capital gripped by worry about Japan's war with Korea and China's involvement, and nobody was willing to see him. He set off again in 1601, with Diego de Pantoja (1571–1618) carrying a clavichord, several clockwork clocks (fascinatingly different and smaller than the water clock in the Forbidden City) and other presents for the emperor. Though the Wanli emperor did not meet Ricci, he conveyed his pleasure at his gifts and ordered that Ricci and De Pantoja stay on in the imperial city to teach the eunuchs how to work the clocks and how to play the clavichord.

The Ming emperors invited another Jesuit, Adam Schall von Bell (1592–1666), to work in the Imperial Calendrical Bureau, translating Western

Father Adam Schall von Bell, who worked as court astronomer at the end of the Ming and then for the conquering Qing emperor. Though the Jesuits were accepted as useful mainly because of their scientific skills, they nevertheless persisted in attempts to convert the inhabitants of the palace.

works on astronomy and mathematics and making new astronomical instruments under the head of the bureau, Xu Guangqi, a Christian convert; but he, too, was kept at a distance from the emperor.[38] He is said to have converted and baptized several eunuchs, including one who took the Christian name of Joseph. Through Joseph's intervention, he first held mass in the Forbidden City in 1632 and in 1634 baptized a further ten eunuchs. Some of the palace ladies saw the religious books he gave to Joseph and requested baptism themselves. Schall von Bell could neither enter the inner palace nor meet them, so he authorized Joseph to conduct the baptism, in which the court ladies took the new names of Agatha, Theodora and Helena, after the saints.[39]

In 1644, when the Ming fell in a short-lived uprising, followed shortly by the arrival of the Manchu banner troops, Schall von Bell stayed on in the stricken city and that same year was appointed Head of the Astronomical Bureau by Prince Dorgon (1612–50), the fourteenth son of Nurhaci (1559–1626), the founder of the Qing dynasty. Dorgon had led the Qing army into Beijing and quickly re-established order and government. Whilst the Ming emperor had kept the Jesuits at arm's length, the new Manchu imperial family positively embraced this useful foreigner, the young Shunzhi emperor (1638–61) even calling him 'Mafu' or Grandpapa.[40]

The Manchu emperors, particularly at the beginning of the dynasty, had a completely different attitude to foreigners from that of the more insular Ming. Their rapid rise to power in their homeland on the northeast edge of China had already led them to make use of Chinese officials to help them govern their ever-expanding territory and they were prepared to use Jesuits, as translators and scientists (astronomers, mathematicians, cannon-makers) and artists (painters, architects, fountain-makers, glass-makers), in the same way. The employment of foreigners and the adoption of many Chinese institutions did not mean that the early Qing emperors were abandoning their Manchu heritage; on the contrary, much recent scholarship has emphasized its significance.[41]

It was not just the relative receptiveness of the early Qing but the increasing interest of European nations in trade with the Far East that led to the arrival of Western envoys in Beijing. In 1655, a Dutch embassy was received in the outer court by the Shunzhi emperor. Further Dutch embassies arrived in the late eighteenth century, the last in 1794–5, led by Isaac Titsingh and a senior member of the Dutch East India Company in Canton, A. E. van Braam Houckgeest.[42]

The Dutch arrived, unwittingly and unfortunately, on the eve of the Chinese New Year when the Board of Rites had already formally 'closed the official seals' indicating the end of official business for the holidays, which lasted a month. Nevertheless, they were summoned to an imperial audience on 12 January 1795. The Qianlong emperor asked them to powder their hair according to current European fashion; he was presumably amused by this strange habit. An early Chinese term used to describe the Dutch (and later the English) was *hong mao* or 'red hairs', but white powder in their wigs must have made the ambassadorial party look like ghosts to the Chinese. 'At 3 a.m. everybody was bustling' but . . .

it was 5 a.m. before we started . . . and after a quarter of an hour's ride we arrived in the Palace . . . We were conducted into a low and dirty room where we found a great many Mandarins [officials]; this was done in order to save us from being exposed so long to the sharp cold in the open air and was a special mark of attention . . . At six o'clock we were conducted outside . . . on a small court between two gates there was a common tent where the Korean ambassadors were warming themselves. Then we emerged on a large, oblong . . . court, at the end of which there was a beautiful brick building [the *Xihua* or West Glorious Gate: the Dutch entered the Forbidden City from the side, not through the Meridian Gate] with three closed gates. The court was full of people; great and small, rich and poor intermingled, pressing and pushing without any distinction, so that we were struck by such a scene of confusion. We had four Mandarins for conductors, who pulled us hither and thither and did not seem to agree amongst themselves about our place.

The French interpreter noted that members of the Korean ambassadors' entourage kept grabbing at the white powdered wigs 'on which the Mandarins

Early envoys to the Qing court remarked upon the splendour of their welcome with finely caparisoned horses and troops drawn up in the great courtyards and crowds of officials, here shown seated upon mats. From *Three Years Travel from Moscow*, the account of an embassy in 1693–5 from Russia to the Kangxi emperor by Evert Ysbrant Ides, 1706.

had insisted' and much of the pushing resulted from the mandarins hitting out at the Koreans to try and get them to stop.[43]

At last, the mandarins pulled the Dutch to the central pathway where we were told to kneel down on the emperor's appearance . . . A little higher were many Tartar and other Ambassadors, then the Koreans, on whom we followed. After half an hour the gates of the Palace opened, from which on either side a throng of people pressed forward; everyone now took his position and shortly afterwards the general silence announced the emperor's arrival. One saw him approaching through the gate, in a chair, numerous servants and Mandarins on common and unsightly horses rode ahead in the greatest confusion . . . Then followed the yellow sedan-chair surrounded by many great mandarins. Where he passed everyone was kneeling; we were also made to kneel, I myself and Mr. Van Braam lying along the road and the other gentlemen behind us. Some mandarins carrying swords who walked a short distance in front of the chair, stopped for a moment in order to look at us; one of these carried a yellow banner. The emperor stopped a while near the Korean Ambassadors and then near us. I held the box [containing his official letter] with both hands as high as my forehead, a mandarin approached me from the chair and accepted the box. Then with uncovered heads we performed the obeisance, bowing our heads nine times to the ground. The emperor addressed me, inquired after my health, whether we were not cold, and which age our prince had obtained; these questions and my answers were interpreted by one of our *linguas* [translators] who on one side was lying behind me. Presently he went on. The chair was very plain and was carried by eight men in yellow coats and a small plume on their caps. The emperor, though well advanced in years [he was 84], had a good and kind appearance and was dressed in black fur. Behind the chair there followed many mandarins and palace attendants, also some soldiers, and the emperor's horses, of a white colour, strong, spirited and fairly tall, but with thick legs and not of an elegant carriage; because they do not curry their horses they were shaggy and rather dirty; over each of them lay a yellow caparison which likewise was nothing to boast of.[44]

In a straggling and unruly crowd, the Dutch were led over the frozen *Zhong Hai* (Middle Sea) where the emperor left his sedan chair and was carried across the ice on a sledge. The Dutch were taken to a lakeside pavilion where 'Imperial breakfast was sent to us':

The Emperor sent us from his table yellow porcelain saucers with small cakes, for which we did obeisance; shortly afterwards he sent again a dish with pieces of game, looking as if they were remnants of gnawed-off bones. They were dumped on the table, but it required another obeisance. Although this was a visible token of his (the Emperor's) affection, it furnished the most conclusive proof of coarseness and lack of civilization.[45]

The Dutch endured several meetings with Ministers, kept waiting for hours whilst servants stared at them and pulled at their clothes, and on 19 January [1795?], van Braam and his nephew set off at 4.30 a.m. to 'salute' the emperor on his way to the *Tai Miao* [Imperial Ancestral Temple, to the east of the Tiananmen] to sacrifice to his ancestors. The young van Braam had left in such a hurry that he still had his curling papers in his hair as he prostrated himself before the emperor, offering the Chinese another strange variation on European hairstyles.

The Qianlong emperor was more relaxed about outsiders within the inner court and the two van Braams were invited to his residence, the *Ningshougong* or Palace of Tranquil Longevity, where the emperor was watching 'theatricals' in the tiny theatre, the Palace of Pleasant Sounds. Next morning, in the *Baohedian* or Hall of Preserving Harmony, which was where the emperors normally greeted tribute-bearers, the emperor offered the Dutch a ritual cup of wine. As he prostrated himself in acknowledgement, van Braam's hat fell off, 'whereupon his Majesty began to laugh and asked him whether he understood Chinese'. Having spent much time in Canton, van Braam replied, 'Bu dong' [I don't understand it], 'and it seemed to amuse the emperor that he answered in Chinese that he did not understand Chinese.'[46]

The irritations of ritual and mutual lack of information continued. The next morning there was no imperial audience because of an eclipse of the sun: the eunuchs were too busy banging drums and clashing cymbals in attempt to 'rescue' the sun, but no-one had told the Dutch, who were up and ready at 2.30 a.m.

Their last view of the emperor came on 27 January 1795 when, ready at 3 a.m. but kept waiting until 5.30 a.m, they lined up again with the Korean ambassadors at the Meridian Gate to prostrate themselves before the emperor as he made his New Year visit to the Temple of Heaven. The weeks of court attendance, of hanging about in sub-zero temperatures in marble courtyards and of lying flat on the frozen ground, brought none of the trading concessions the Dutch had requested. These Westerners who presented themselves before the emperor did so in the company of Korean ambassadors who made biannual trips to China to 'present tribute' and acknowledge the superiority of the Chinese emperor. Similar tribute delegations arrived on a regular basis from Central Asia, the Mongol regions, Japan and Southeast Asian countries, all accepting the 'superiority' of China. Though Western ambassadors were aware of the tribute system, and the Dutch in particular accepted the ritual of submission, the expansionist mercantile nations of Europe pressed for diplomatic relations as they understood them, on a basis of equality and freedom to trade as they wished. These, the Chinese of the eighteenth century and their Manchu rulers were not prepared to grant.

3

Banquets and bedchambers

The wide open spaces of the Outer Court had huge ceremonial halls raised high on white marble platforms, built to overawe the officials and tribute-bearing ambassadors who entered its great red gate. These give way to the smaller, lower, tightly-packed buildings of the Inner Court behind the Gate of Heavenly Purity.

Cut off by a wide courtyard and a high red wall, the Inner Court saw much more building and many other changes than the Outer Court. When the number of concubines or imperial princes rose, more buildings had to be constructed to accommodate them. Though many of the larger halls had assigned functions, these were sometimes changed. A hall might be abandoned for a while if an emperor had died in it, or an emperor (or an empress dowager) might decide to change residence on reaching the auspicious age of sixty.

The central axis of the Inner Court has three halls, paralleling the three main halls of the Outer Court. The first, inside the Gate of Heavenly Purity, is the Palace of Heavenly Purity. A large, nine-bay building, this was the residence of the emperor throughout the Ming and early Qing. The Yongzheng emperor (r. 1723–35) decided to move his residence to the Hall of Mental Cultivation immediately to the west of the Palace of Heavenly Purity, though he continued to use the Palace of Heavenly Purity as a study and office for receiving foreign emissaries, bringing government into his private quarters and displaying, like many of the Qing emperors, a more casual attitude to the division between the Inner and Outer Palaces.[47] The Palace of Heavenly Purity remained an important official building throughout the Qing, though the emperor no longer slept there. The galleries around the courtyard housed an office of the Hanlin academy, the highest scholarly institution in China, where scholars remained on duty to answer any imperial queries. It also housed the Imperial Wardrobe, the Imperial Apothecary – with eunuch doctors on duty night and day – the duty room of the head eunuch and the Office of the Treasury.

Behind the Palace of Heavenly Purity was the Hall of Union, built during the Ming. Placed between the emperor's official residence and that of the empress (in the Palace of Earthly Tranquillity behind), it was used at festival times when the

A silver seal made for the Commissioner of the Office of Transmission, dated 1749. Memorials could not move through the palace without his permission and his seal served as a 'signature'. Imperial seals were carefully guarded and securely stored as emblems of imperial rule.

The Xuantong emperor, Henry Aisin-Gioro Puyi, last of the Qing rulers, shown in Western-style military uniform. After fleeing from the Forbidden City in 1924, he took refuge in Tianjin but was persuaded by the Japanese invaders to serve as their 'emperor' in Manchuria in 1934. He rehabilitated himself and worked in the botanical gardens in Beijing, dying in 1967.

court paid homage to the empress. Its significant central position meant that it was chosen by the Qianlong emperor as the place to store the imperial seals in cabinets with yellow silk covers. Seals had a great significance in China, being used from a very early period to authenticate documents.

Behind the Hall of Union was the Palace of Earthly Tranquillity, built in the Ming as the residence of the empress and preserved as such during the Qing, although none actually lived there. A heated room at the eastern end of the Palace, with a brick *kang* which could be kept warm with braziers underneath, was used from time to time as the imperial nuptial hall: the Kangxi, Tongzhi, Guangxu and Xuantong emperors spent their honeymoons there, moving to the east or west palaces after three days. The wedding night of the Xuantong emperor (Puyi) in 1922 was not a success. He had not previously met his bride. 'The empress came into my field of vision with a crimson satin cloth embroidered with a dragon and phoenix over her head', at which point he became vaguely curious as to what the bride arranged for him looked like. He said of the bridal room,

It was unfurnished except for the bed-platform which filled about a quarter of it, and everything except the floor was red. When we had drunk the nuptial cup and eaten sons-and-grandsons' cakes and entered this dark room I felt stifled. The bride sat on the bed, her head bent down. I looked around me and saw that everything was red: red bed-curtains, red pillows, a red dress, a red skirt, red flowers and a red face . . . it all looked like a melted red wax candle. I did not know whether to stand or sit, decided I preferred the Mind Nurture Palace, and went back there.[48]

A corner of a domestic courtyard to the rear of the Forbidden City. In marked contrast to the tall, imposing main halls, the domestic buildings were often simple, small constructions, with lattice windows and narrow side wings. Here, impressive eave decorations are seen on a small building, with a flower bed set in the courtyard.

The imperial marriage bed was set in an alcove and bordered by an openwork timber curtain screen. It is still hung with red silk curtains embroidered with 'one hundred children at play', a familiar design from painting and porcelain which (like the sons-and-grandsons' cakes) was intended to ensure numerous progeny, as long as the emperor did what was expected of him and stayed with his new bride. The interior of the Palace of Earthly Tranquillity is plainer than other halls and during the Qing was used for worship and sacrifice, with stoves ready to cook offerings made to the various Manchu gods.

The Hall of Mental Cultivation, west of the Palace of Heavenly Purity, was used as an imperial residence by the Yongzheng emperor who, on accession, was unwilling to move into the palace where his father had lived and worked for over sixty years. Built as a princely rather than an imperial residence, it is smaller and more intimate, more of a domestic than an imperial building. The rear wall is lined with dark wooden bookshelves, their contents protected with blue silk curtains. The west room is known as the 'Room of Three Rarities' because the Qianlong emperor used to keep here precious rubbings of the calligraphy of the three Wangs: Wang Xizhi (307–65), his son Wang Xianzhi (344–88) and nephew Wang Shun (350–401).[49] The floor of the front part of the room is covered with blue and white tiles, almost Dutch in appearance, whose pattern is echoed in a large *trompe l'oeil* painting made in 1765 by the court artist Jin Tingbao and the Italian Jesuit Giuseppe Castiglione. The east chamber, quite plainly decorated with more blue silk curtained bookcases, was where the Yongzheng emperor would summon his ministers for discussion but, later in the Qing, it was where the Empress Dowager Cixi (1835–1908) dictated government affairs from behind a yellow silk curtain, hidden behind the emperor's throne. Cixi acted as regent during the minority of her son the Tongzhi emperor and, on his death in 1874, she selected another minor as the Guangxu emperor so that she could remain behind her silk curtain ordering the affairs of the state.

Behind the main Hall of Mental Cultivation, a corridor leads to a parallel hall where the Yongzheng emperor slept. Most of the rooms have *kang* beds for warmth in winter and are quite simply furnished. The eastern room, known as the Hall of Manifest Compliance, is where the empress stayed whenever she slept with the emperor. The 'delivery' of concubines to the emperor has been described in detail by late Qing eunuchs, though we have no way of knowing if the process was the same during the Ming. In the late nineteenth century, after dinner, the eunuch in charge of the imperial bedchamber would offer the emperor a silver salver containing the names of his favourite concubines. If the emperor selected one, he would turn the tablet face down. Another eunuch was then dispatched to fetch the concubine and carry her on his back, naked in a feather quilt, to the imperial chamber. He would wait a specified time and then shout 'Time's up!' three times before collecting the concubine. If the emperor wanted her to have a child, the date was recorded; otherwise the unfortunate woman was dosed with contraceptive potions such as the 'cold flower'.[50]

The imperial women and imperial children lived in the six Eastern and six Western Palaces, clusters of dwellings with halls and galleries surrounding an open courtyard closed off by a gate. Apart from their yellow-tiled roofs and lavish interiors, these did not differ much from grand houses in the outer city of Beijing. There was considerable movement between these two groups of palaces: the Empress Dowager Cixi moved into the Western Palace of Gathering Excellence on her fiftieth birthday in 1884 and stayed there for ten years before moving over

The Empress Dowager Cixi is carried by her strongest eunuchs in a sedan chair with embroidered parasol overhead. The decorations in her hair and her high white platform soles, worn by all Manchu women, can be clearly seen. Such photographs were part of a move to modernity, forced upon the palace by the Boxer rebellion of 1900.

to the Eastern Palace of Tranquil Longevity, the Qianlong emperor's retirement retreat. The Qianlong emperor lived in the narrow courtyard of the Palace of Blessing on the east side of the inner court but in 1727, when he married, he followed his father's orders and moved to the Abode of the Hidden Dragon in the northwest corner of the Forbidden City. After his elevation from prince to last emperor, Puyi moved into the Eastern Palace where most of the young Qing princes lived as children, and had his lessons in the Palace of Bringing Forth Blessings, but as a young adult he stayed in the Palace of Mental Cultivation on the western side of the Forbidden City.

In the Western Palace complex, the Hall of Gathering Excellence, redecorated for Cixi's fiftieth birthday, was built in 1420, when it was known as the Hall of

Framed openwork pictures of flowers made from strips of dark iron reveal a more restrained taste than some of the decorations in the Forbidden City. Silhouettes of chrysanthemums, lilies and rocks, recalling monochrome brushwork, were made to hang in domestic rooms.

Longevity and Prosperity. The interior decoration is Victorian, with dark and heavy carved hardwood furniture including a dark screen with mirror panels and screen doors with silk paintings set between long glass panes. Plate glass and silver-backed mirrors were Western introductions into nineteenth century China, where windows had been traditionally made of lattice pasted with paper and where mirrors were small discs of highly polished bronze. The Empress Dowager Cixi was interested in Western fashions so, apart from the technical innovations, it is likely that her taste in furniture had been influenced by contemporary European styles. The outer eaves of the hall are painted with 'Suzhou-style' paintings, characteristically used in the Forbidden City for women's apartments. Birds, flowers and landscape scenes (the latter also owing something to the newly introduced Western perspective), scrolling plum blossom and speckled bamboo designs lighten the buildings in which the women lived, and set them apart from the more formal designs on the eaves of the outer court.

Next to Cixi's Palace of Gathering Excellence is the Palace of Eternal Spring where the concubine Lady Li lived in the late Ming. Lady Li began work in the Ming Forbidden City as a serving maid in the entourage of the Prince of Yu. She bore him his first son (the Wanli emperor) and, after he became the Longqing emperor in 1567, was given the title empress dowager. Though she held great power when her son became emperor in 1572 at the age of nine, she was believed never to have abused it, treating the young emperor strictly, 'personally arousing him from sleep in the morning and supervising his attire and behaviour', compelling him to attend court audiences and hearing his lessons herself.[51]

Apart from the exterior, little remains from the Ming, since the palace was used by Cixi before she moved to the Palace of Gathering Excellence, as well as by the concubines of the Guangxu emperor (r. 1875–1908) and Puyi. The interior is filled with the same sort of dark Victorian furniture seen elsewhere in the Western Palaces, as well as semi-Western style paintings of scenes from the eighteenth-century novel *Hongloumeng* (Dream of the Red Chamber / Story of the Stone) which dates from the Guangxu period.

Within the walls of the Forbidden City, only the emperor led a regulated life, dictated by his work. The emperors ate twice a day, the Yongle emperor taking lunch of white noodles, fresh pickles, bean curd, dried meats and fish at noon. On ordinary days, when there were no banquets or guests for a meal, it is thought that the Ming emperors may have taken their main meals with their family, including women.[52] When the Ming emperors held great banquets in the outer court, there were often parallel banquets, with female musicians, held by the empresses in the Palace of Earthly Tranquillity.

The Qianlong emperor (r. 1736–99) rose at 6 a.m. and ate his first meal, prepared in a nearby kitchen, at 8 a.m. His second meal of the day was at 2 p.m. At night he might take a little light refreshment before retiring. In a break with the Ming tradition, the Qing emperors did not generally eat with their family, nor usually with anyone else at all, though the Qianlong emperor sometimes invited a consort to dinner (and presumably for the night). This was partly because protocol dictated that everyone, except a dowager empress, had to stand in the emperor's presence, which would have made eating uncomfortable.[53]

Serving the emperor separately would also have made it easier to take the customary elaborate precautions against poison, such as the use of silver bowls or strips of silver said to indicate the presence of poison by changing colour, and the practice of eunuchs tasting everything first. It was also easier to serve one person in the Manchu style, which differed from Chinese practice:

The Chinese place the bowls of food, one at a time, in the centre of the table, and everyone eats out of these bowls, sticking their chopsticks in and helping themselves to what they want. The Manchus eat quite differently and are served with individual bowls and dishes, the same as in any other country. Her Majesty [Cixi] was very proud of this and said that it saved time, not to mention being cleaner.[54]

Different emperors had different tastes. The Kangxi emperor (r. 1662–1722) extolled the simple life: 'the best thing for health is to eat and drink carefully and rise and retire at regular hours', and recommended avoidance of cold food when ill and roast meat at all times: 'fowl, mutton and pork should be boiled or stewed'.[55] Kangxi said he loved vegetables and fish, and the Guangxu emperor (r. 1875–1908) was said to breakfast simply on milk, rice porridge and wheat cakes. Amongst the vast number of records surviving in the Imperial Archives is the menu of one of the Qianlong emperor's meals in 1754, including a dish of fat chicken, boiled duck and bean curd, swallows' nests and shredded smoked duck, clear soup, a dish of shredded stewed chicken, a dish of smoked fat chicken and Chinese cabbage, a dish of salted duck and pork, court-style fried chicken, dishes of bamboo-stuffed steamed dumplings, rice cakes and rice cakes with honey. The meal was accompanied by pickled aubergine, Chinese cabbage pickled in brine and cucumbers marinated in soy sauce, served in a special ceramic container decorated with hollyhock flowers.[56]

This is a simple meal compared with the 'hundred dishes' said to have been prepared for the Empress Dowager Cixi on a twice-daily basis. One of the difficulties of feeding the emperor was that there was no fixed place in which he might eat: his food was brought to him wherever he happened to be. Thus, 'when the emperor was taking a walk, men of the refreshment division had to follow him with two round bamboo baskets, containing plenty of refreshments, tea and a small stove so that food might be ready within minutes after it was ordered.'[57]

It is possible that the relative restraint of the meals served in private, particularly to the early Qing emperors, reflected their antagonism to what they saw as the decadence of the (Chinese) Ming dynasty. For these emperors, the 'wide robes and flowing sleeves', innumerable eunuchs and the excesses of the table of the late Ming emperors were in stark contrast with the Manchu traditions of riding, hunting and archery, underpinning a healthy, plain-living, open-air life. The Kangxi emperor wrote lyrically of the joys of the hunt, of days spent in the open air to 'refresh the spirit': 'there is tea, made from fresh snow on a little brazier slung between two horses. There is the perfect flavour of bream and carp

Formal portrait of the Qianlong emperor in court robe, Qing dynasty. Qing robes differed from those of the Ming, with high collars, cross-over fastenings and 'horse-shoe' cuffs.

from the mountain streams, caught by oneself in the early morning . . . There is venison, roasted over an open fire by a tent pitched on the sunny slope of a mountain; or the liver of a newly-killed stag, cooked with one's own hands (even if the rain is falling), and eaten with salt and vinegar.'[58]

The early Qing emperors remained fond of many Manchu dishes, such as freshly caught venison, and were very keen on cakes. In one respect they were remarkably different from the Ming emperors and all other Chinese, for they drank their tea with milk. The Qianlong emperor drank tea with his two main meals, often with milk, and special herds of cows were kept, with 100 cows reserved to provide milk for the emperor, twenty-four for the empress dowager and so on down through the ranks.[59] There were Manchu dishes that changed subtly over the decades, such as *za*. This derived from a simple dish made from local ingredients when the Qing army camped near the Great Wall on 5 July 1619, during the Campaign of Conquest. Nurhaci enjoyed a meal of dove minced with rice and wrapped in cabbage leaves, and it was eaten every year on the same day in commemoration. By Cixi's time, over three hundred years later, the dove meat was no longer simply roasted but fully seasoned.

There was only ever one emperor at a time in the Forbidden City; for women the situation was different. There were three major groups in the inner palace: imperial consorts (empresses and concubines); 'royal princesses', that is women related to the imperial family who, unless married, could not respectably live outside the inner palace; and palace servants of many different sorts, some of whom might move up into the superior categories. Imperial consorts were carefully chosen; in the Ming, often from close associates of the imperial family such as the Yongle emperor's wife, Empress Xu, the eldest daughter of Xu Da (1332–85), who had fought side by side with Yongle's father from 1353. Through failure to bear a son or through death (Xu died in 1407), they were often supplanted by secondary wives drawn from the ranks of concubines or palace servants chosen for their looks rather than their connections.

The Qing emperors also had carefully chosen wives. Forbidden to marry Chinese, Qing imperial wives were selected mainly from the families of high-ranking Manchu bannermen or, especially in the early days, from allies such as various Mongol groups. One of the secondary wives of Abahai (1592–1643), eighth son of Nurhaci, was Borjigid-shi (1613–87), a descendant of Genghis Khan, whose spirit was sometimes invoked by the Qing. She gave birth to Nurgaci's ninth and youngest son, who was later chosen as his heir (and reigned as the Shunzhi emperor, 1644–61). The surprising choice of a ninth son, aged only five, was the result of a compromise made by the ruling council. Borjigid-shi is said to have initiated 'the Qing institution of female influence from "behind the screen" that was later used by the Empress Dowager Cixi'.[60]

Though relations with her son deteriorated, Borjigid-shi was very close to one grandson, the third son of the Shunzhi emperor. When the emperor lay dying of smallpox, a disease to which the Manchus and Mongols were particularly susceptible, his third son was selected as his heir, largely because he had survived an attack of smallpox and was thus immune. The Chinese, who knew how to inoculate against smallpox (by breathing in tiny pieces of infected skin), were largely immune,[61] and the Kangxi emperor later followed the Chinese practice, saying of his troops that he 'had them inoculated as I did my children'.[62]

The young Kangxi emperor, only seven when he succeeded, was largely brought up by Borjigid-shi after his mother died, which gave her further opportunity for control from behind the screen.[63] Borjigid-shi is one amongst many examples of women within the Forbidden City whose status was raised through bearing a son and through influence on heirs-apparent. One group of women that rose to surprising prominence in the Ming was the imperial wet-nurses who, if the child they fed grew up to become emperor, were given honorary titles and became noblewomen.[64]

Forty wet-nurses, and eighty substitutes, were employed within the Forbidden City. In the month when an imperial infant was expected, a selected group was gathered; but the final choice had to wait until the baby appeared because it was customary to choose a wet-nurse who had a girl of her own for an imperial son and vice versa, perhaps to match the yin and yang or protect the

Timbers throughout the Forbidden City were painted to protect them against the elements. Decorative ceilings were an imperial luxury, forbidden to all but the highest officials. This ceiling, with its floral motifs and range of colours, was for a hall inhabited by women.

imperial child in some way (it would certainly have prevented substitution). When they were working, wet-nurses received an allowance of rice and about five ounces of meat a day, coal in cold weather and an annual clothing allowance.[65]

The wet-nurse of the Tianqi emperor (r. 1621–28), Lady Ke, was particularly powerful. The emperor gave her the title 'holy mother', a large house, many jewels and official posts to her son and brother. She was allowed to ride in a sedan chair within the palace, a privilege normally reserved for imperial consorts. He also approved of her 'vegetarian' (sexless) marriage with Wei Zhongxian, a eunuch, but her power within the court aroused jealousy and the moment the emperor died, she was beaten to death in the eunuch-run laundry service, on the order of Tianqi's younger brother.[66]

In any reign during the Ming, there were said to be between fifty and a hundred 'imperial women' and 2,000 and 3,000 palace women.[67] They included female sedan-chair carriers, dancers, musicians, physicians, accountants and general servants. Most were recruited in groups of 40 to 500 and selected according to their merits, but there were forced recruitments, notably during the reign of the Jiaqing emperor (r. 1522–67). He ordered the recruitment of 760 girls aged between eight and fourteen in 1547, 1552 and 1555, believing that very young sexual partners would enhance his vigour.[68] Most palace serving women were released when they were too ill or too old to be of any use, though sometimes natural phenomena like comet showers were interpreted as an excess of 'yin' or female essence, provoking large-scale dismissals of palace women to correct the balance.

Women seem to have moved up and down between the positions of palace servant and imperial consort. Even if a palace woman bore a son, her position was

not necessarily secure. The eldest son of the Xuande emperor, born in 1427, was the son of an unknown serving woman of Lady Sun. Lady Sun took the child and claimed it as her own so that she could be elevated to the position of empress, deposing the childless Lady Hu. Similarly, the empress Lady Zhang brought up the future Zhengde emperor (r. 1506–21) as her own son, though his real mother was a minor, seventh–grade consort, Zhang Huanger. Zhang Huanger tried to protest but was demoted from imperial consort to the palace service and her father was executed.[69]

Lady Ji, born in a 'barbarian tribe' in far southwestern Guangxi province, was brought to the palace as a child captive. She was highly intelligent and was given work as a clerk in the imperial library. The Chenghua emperor (r. 1465–87) saw her in the palace grounds and visited her that night. Her pregnancy roused the jealousy of the powerful consort Lady Wan. She had looked after the emperor since he was two, massaged his stomach pains, dressed up as a soldier, which he found greatly attractive, and, despite being seventeen years older, bore the emperor his first son (who died in childhood) in 1466. Lady Wan had Lady Ji imprisoned in the Hall of Tranquillity and Happiness which, despite its name, was the 'cold palace', a place of internal exile for discarded palace women within the Forbidden City. Helped by the Empress Wu, also banished by Lady Wan, and a eunuch, Zhang Min, Lady Ji gave birth to the emperor's only son.

The child, later to reign as the Hongzhi emperor (1488–1505), was finally presented to his father and Lady Ji was brought back to the Palace of Eternal Life and given the title Virtuous Imperial Concubine. She died shortly afterwards and, at the same time, the eunuch Zhang Min committed suicide by swallowing gold. Both may have been victims of Lady Wan.[70]

LEFT Blue and white porcelain vase with ring handles, Zhengde reign period (1506–21). The porcelain of the period, made in the southern ceramic centre of Jingdezhen, was characterized by fine blue and white wares but the emperor himself was described as eccentric, drunk and neglectful of his duties.

Double-gourd vase, Jiajing reign period, 1521–67. The Jiajing emperor believed in Taoism. Imperial ceramics of the period often show Taoist influence in form and in decoration, and the deity of longevity and the eight Taoist immortals are depicted here.

The Jiaqing emperor (r. 1522–67) was notoriously cruel to his consorts: more than two hundred are said to have died as a result of beatings. In 1542 sixteen consorts, led by Yang Jinying, tried to strangle him in his sleep. Unfortunately, the knot they tied in a silken cord failed to tighten as they pulled it, and the emperor woke up. Yang Jinying stabbed him in the eye with her silver hairpin. The empress rushed to the rescue and the sixteen girls were punished with the utmost severity, their bodies cut to pieces and their heads exposed on poles. Ten of their relatives were also executed (in the Chinese justice system, family responsibility is a serious matter) and twenty were made slaves. The emperor lost his eye and, conscious of his disfigurement, never left the inner palace again, refusing to attend audiences.[71]

The Yongle emperor also dealt cruelly with insubordination. In 1421 some 2,800 serving-women were tortured to admit rebellion and then sliced to death. This massacre was the result of a long-standing series of intrigues amongst the palace women led by a minor consort, Lady Lu, who finally committed suicide when her 'adulterous' relationship with a eunuch was discovered.[72]

In the early Ming some palace women were subject to a final horror, being chosen to 'accompany' the emperor to the tomb. Sixteen women were buried with the Yongle emperor, seven with Hongxi and eight with the Xuande emperor. An account of the deaths of Yongle's consorts was recorded in the Korean annals:

A bugle announced the time for them to enter the room . . . The women were forced to stand on chairs and hang themselves by ropes tied to the ceiling. They would die in pain when the eunuchs removed the chairs . . . Two Korean consorts, Lady Han and Lady Cui, were also required to die. The chair under Lady Han was removed so abruptly that she did not have time to say goodbye to her nanny.[73]

Some Korean palace women fared slightly better. The Xuande emperor was very keen on all things Korean, sending his first demand to the king of Korea in 1426 for virgins, eunuchs and female cooks. The Korean king personally made the first selection of seven virgins, ten cooks, sixteen palace maids and ten young eunuchs. When Xuande died, fifty-three Korean women were sent back to Korea, at their request.[74]

A later 'foreign' consort in the Forbidden City was Rong fei (Fragrant concubine), a Uighur woman from eastern Turkestan who became a fourth-rank consort of the Qianlong emperor in 1760, rising to second rank in 1768.[75] When tribute gifts of Hami melon from the oases of Turkestan were presented, she was given more than the other ladies, in acknowledgement of her origins. She was allowed to wear Uighur dress and had her own cook to prepare spiced rice pilaf with mutton, carrots and other vegetables fried with onion. A painting in the imperial collection shows Rong fei, her hair in the long plaits of a Uighur woman, holding an arrow and riding a dappled horse alongside the Qianlong emperor as he shoots a stag with his bow.[76]

Another striking portrait, very characteristic of the Qianlong emperor's interest in foreign artistic styles, depicts a woman holding a sword and wearing European armour with a plumed helmet. This is often assumed to be a portrait of Rong fei by the Jesuit Giuseppe Castiglione. The image may have contributed to the legends that grew up around the 'Fragrant concubine' in the late Qing. Though her family supported the conquest of Turkestan, she was turned into a figure of resistance, said to have refused the emperor and to have carried a knife until she was forced to commit suicide by the emperor's mother. In fact, court archives record Rong fei as having a peaceful life in the Forbidden City, ordering silks, taking medicine and eating milk cakes and tangerines presented by the emperor.[77]

The best-known woman to inhabit the Forbidden City (though she greatly preferred the summer palace, Yiheyuan) was the Empress Dowager Cixi (1835–1908). Yehenara (or Yehonala) was born into a family of the Bordered Blue Banner and selected at the age of seventeen *sui*[78] as a low-ranking consort. The birth of her son raised her status and title and, when her son succeeded his father in 1861, the eight regents entrusted with running the affairs of state were compelled to seek the consent of Cixi and the Empress Cian before issuing edicts. The two women held the official seals, Cian the seal to be affixed at the beginning of each edict and Cixi (on behalf of her son) the seal for the end of the edict. In 1881, Cian died and Cixi became sole regent.

Preparations for the birth that was to raise Cixi's status are recorded in the Imperial Archive. In the sixth month of her pregnancy, according to custom, her mother was summoned. Six maids, two midwives and six doctors were appointed. Bolts of Korean cotton in blue and white, unbleached cottons and silks were ordered to make up '27 jackets (18 cotton padded and 9 lined), four short gowns, 75 bed sheets . . . four stomachers, two makeshift curtains, 18 quilts, 12 mattresses of varying sizes, two bags filled with bran, four bands and one door curtain.'[79] Two wooden tubs, two wooden bowls, a shovel, small knife and a large black felt blanket were provided, as well as an 'auspicious' cradle, and, in early April, her doctors requested 'a childbirth-hastening stone'.[80] Other preparations included the preparation of a small pit, dug by eunuchs, in which the afterbirth and other discarded objects would be buried. When the pit was ready, the two midwives sang good luck songs and threw in pieces of red silk, gold and silver ingots and a pair of chopsticks. The word for chopsticks in Chinese, *kuaizi*, is a pun for 'quickly [delivered of a] boy'. Two weeks before the birth, the chief eunuch brought a sword from the Hall of Mental Cultivation to hang on the wall and scare away evil spirits. The first son of the emperor was delivered after a labour of about four hours on 27 April 1856. According to the Imperial Household Regulations and Cixi's status as a consort, 200 taels (a Chinese weight, like an ingot) of silver and 40 bolts of dress silk were due to her, but the Xianfeng emperor gave her 300 taels and 70 bolts of first-class silk.[81]

A great deal is known about the daily life of Cixi in old age, particularly from an account written by one of her ladies in waiting, 'Princess' Der Ling, the daughter of a Manchu, Yugeng, who had served as minister (ambassador) to

大清國當今聖母皇太后萬歲萬歲萬萬歲

The Empress Dowager Cixi with Western diplomats' wives, showing off her openwork pearl vest, pearl-hung hat, embroidered gown and Manchu platform shoes. The foreign guests have to stand in her presence.

Japan and France. Cixi selected Der Ling and her sister for palace service as she was curious about foreign customs and fashions.[82]

Der Ling, like all palace women, had to stand in Cixi's presence, even when eating, which she found extremely tiring, and the constant kowtowing to acknowledge any favour made her dizzy. Der Ling's first duty in the morning was to make Cixi's bed. Cixi slept in her underwear, and when she rose, eunuchs took her bedding outside to air it.

A eunuch brushed Cixi's hair, pulling it up into a tight top-knot to which the wide Manchu headdress was pinned. Cixi then washed her face with perfumed soap and sprayed it with a solution made of honey and flower petals before putting on pink powder. Pulling on her white silk socks, a pale pink shirt and a short silk under-gown embroidered with bamboo leaves, she looked over a selection of dresses brought in by her maids. Der Ling describes her choosing a sea-green dress embroidered all over with white storks; then a silver stork, set with pearls, to pin in her hair, and a mauve short-jacket, also embroidered with storks. 'Her handkerchief and shoes were also embroidered with storks and when she was entirely dressed she looked like the stork lady.' Her shoes, worn by all Manchu ladies, were embroidered slippers on high white platforms, in her case often with dangling strings of pearls.

Like the emperors, Cixi 'took her meals wherever she happened to be, so that there was no particular place that she used as a dining room . . . There were about one hundred and fifty different kinds of food, for I counted them.'[83]

Many of the early Qing emperors were long-lived, as was Cixi, who died at the age of seventy-five. In their death rituals, the Manchus added many distinctive Manchu touches to the Chinese ceremonials that had been observed by the Ming. According to Confucius, 'to be filial was "to serve parents according to the rights when they are alive, bury them according to the rites when they die, and sacrifice to them according to the rites thereafter."'[84] From 1424, the Ming emperors and their empresses and consorts were buried with expensive grave goods in a tomb enclosure outside Beijing.[85]

In their northeastern homeland, different Manchu groups carried out very different burials, including water burial and tree 'burial'.[86] The ancestors of the Qing emperors were cremated, but after 1661 all the emperors and almost all their wives, consorts and children were buried in three separate tomb enclosures, marking a major and permanent change in Manchu ritual. In many ways the funerals of Qing emperors were similar to those of the Ming, although many of their grave goods, the articles which they had used when alive, were not buried with them but burnt, along with paper money and paper models (such as everyday articles, vehicles and servants). The body, washed and dressed in the most formal form of court dress, was wrapped in five covers, woven with Buddhist incantations, and a further eight shrouds of satin woven with dragons. It was placed in a nanmu cedarwood coffin which, after two weeks lying in state, was sealed in forty-nine coats of plain lacquer covered in gold lacquer.

An imperial funeral procession with the coffin in the centre. Personal possessions as well as daily necessities were also carried in the procession to accompany the soul on its journey. It might take days to reach the imperial burial ground and burials took place often months after death, awaiting an auspicious day.

Like the first Ming emperor, who felt that emotion was paramount in mourning, various of the Qing emperors showed special favour to those they had specially loved. The Kangxi emperor mourned his grandmother Borgijid-shi as a parent, rather than a grandmother, declaring that for the full twenty-seven months he would wear cotton mourning clothes (rather than raw silk) and cancelling the New Year festivities. He cut off his queue (the plait that hung down his back) in the traditional Manchu sign of bereavement. When the Qianlong emperor's first wife, Empress Xiaoxian, died in 1748 of a malarial fever, the emperor decreed that all marriages, listening to music or participating in any form of entertainment were forbidden to all his officials throughout the country for the full 100 days. He also expected that none of his officials would shave their heads or faces for the same period. Jiang Xinghan, a First Captain in the Shandong Green Standards, shaved within the 100 days and was beheaded, and two other high officials were subsequently executed in the 'shaving scandal'.[87]

During the Qing, the actual burial might take place long after death, even after the official mourning period was over: the Qianlong emperor's mother was finally buried in the imperial tomb enclosure three years after her death. Her funeral procession, following the immense catafalque which would take many weeks to reach the tomb, included:

camels and horses, two by two, loaded with provisions as if for a long trip: beds, utensils, provisions, etc . . . carts . . . sedan chairs, armchairs, chairs, stools, cushions, trunks, basins, and all the articles of the toilette. All this marches in file for twenty-eight rows . . . jewels, mirrors, fans, etc . . . were carried separately by the servants, forming several ranks, after which was carried, with much respect, the little stick which she used during her old age.[88]

Garden parties

Gardens had been important to the rulers of China for thousands of years. When Yongle built his palace he retained the lake gardens that ran along the west side of the Forbidden City proper, first dug out by the Jin two hundred years earlier. The long series of three lakes, or 'seas', fed by the Jinshui (Golden river), saw constant rebuilding and improvement through the Yuan, Ming and Qing, with the construction of artificial islands, bridges, pavilions and temples, but always retaining a naturalistic appearance with rock-lined shores overhung by willows.

The smaller, courtyard gardens within the Forbidden City itself are different in style, reflecting the smaller, enclosed, inner-city gardens that were a feature of elegant life in the Ming and Qing. The main garden at the very back of the Forbidden City, on the central axis, just inside the Shengwu gate, was known as the 'Rear Garden' in the Ming. Many of the ancient trees, such as the old cypress, junipers, catalpas and the Chinese scholar trees were planted during the Ming.[89] It is in many ways a formal garden, with a central building surrounded by

The small 'Half acre garden' in Beijing was a model 'scholar's garden with elegant buildings, trees, a pool, rockery and specimen plants and ornamental rocks on stands.' The small imperial gardens within the Forbidden City followed the same aesthetic. From Linqing's memoirs, 1847–50.

bamboos, cypresses and the Hall of Imperial Tranquillity, where the emperors came on New Year's Day to sacrifice to a Taoist water god thought to be one of the many protectors against fire within the Forbidden City.[90] The pavilions flanking the hall, and other buildings in the garden, are all roofed with yellow tiles and their timbers are painted red with highly decorative painting under the eaves which make the garden more cheerful in the long Beijing winter.

The Rear Garden is entered through a small gate, the First Gate to Heaven, through which a pair of entwined junipers are visible, their trunks trained around each other in a life-sized version of the sort of training often seen in Chinese *pencai* (Japanese bonsai) or 'pot-grown' specimens. Against the west wall is a small two-storey house, which the last emperor's Scottish tutor, Reginald Johnston, used as a study in 1924.

Its name was . . . 'Lodge of the Nourishment of Nature'. My generous host caused it to be furnished for me in European style – though had I been consulted I should have preferred Chinese furniture – and I added to its attractions by bringing in a quantity of books from my own library. It contained several sitting rooms and a bedroom. Next door, rooms were provided for my own servants or for those of the palace servants who were told to wait on me. There I spent the greater part of each day, sometimes alone with my books, sometimes in the emperor's company. Occasionally he would invite himself for lunch in my pavilion, on which occasions the materials for the feast were always brought by servants from his own kitchen.

There, Reginald Johnston introduced Puyi to the Bengali poet Rabindranath Tagore and the last descendant of the Qing imperial family, the Marquis of Extended Grace, who graciously acknowledged Ming supremacy whilst continuing to carry out his ceremonial duties to his ancestors in the Ming tomb enclosure.[91]

Regularly placed, rectangular flowerbeds were planted with tree peonies and there were white marble raised beds in the form of lozenges or fans. Many of the stone-flagged paths in the garden are bordered with 'pavement pictures' made from coloured pebbles, depicting flowers, animals, scenes from opera and landscapes.[92]

Throughout the garden were elaborately carved marble plinths displaying fantastic rocks, described as *penjing* or 'pot scenes' (more commonly flat basins with single small rocks planted with dwarf plants and surrounded by water to create a miniature mountain scene). The extraordinary rocks selected for this special display reflect a development in 'petromania' since the time of the Huizong emperor of the Song who was famous for collecting garden rocks.[93]

There is the 'sea cucumber stone', a seething mass of fossilized sea cucumbers (a delicacy when not fossilized), patterned marble, fossilized sponges and stones that look like fossilized waves. Another stone, said to look like a man bowing with bended knees, is entitled 'Zhuge Liang [181–234, a semi-legendary military hero] bowing to the meteorites of the Big Dipper'.[94] Inscribing things was a way of showing respect for them, and the Qianlong emperor loved to demonstrate his connoisseurship by inscribing paintings and rocks.

On the east side of the gate in the back wall is a high piled rockery, the Hill of Piled Excellence, with a pavilion on a high terrace on the top. Constructed on the orders of the Wanli emperor (r. 1573–1620) to offer a fine view of the garden, it had a far greater significance for the palace women who were never allowed out, for they could climb up and get a glimpse of the world outside the Forbidden City. The last emperor and his tutor climbed up to peer through field-glasses at the warlords' troops massed behind the Forbidden City during an attempted *coup d'état* in 1924.[95] At the mid-autumn festival families climbed hills to view the full moon and eat moon cakes, and the imperial family climbed up to the Hall of Piled Excellence to view the moon like everyone else. On the ninth day of the ninth month, the Double Ninth festival, they would return with a jug of chrysanthemum wine and a bag of wheat cakes to commemorate an escape from plague in the Han dynasty.[96]

The other gardens within the Forbidden City were built during the reign of the Qianlong emperor. The Palace of Compassion and Tranquillity, on the western axis of the Forbidden City (where dowager empresses and consorts lived), was built in 1536, rebuilt during the reign of the Wanli emperor and altered in 1769. The long enclosure, with a rockery inside the main gate, has main halls far to the rear and the rest of the space is tranquil. It includes a small central pavilion with tanked pools on either side, and is planted with gingkos, Chinese parasol trees, cypresses and flowering prunus to provide a grassy and natural effect.

The garden of the Palace for Establishing Happiness, built in 1740, is really just a massive rockery with trees. It is set in front of a series of linked buildings in the northwest of the Forbidden City and provides an elegant view from the Pavilion of Extended Spring in a relatively cramped site. The buildings burned down in slightly mysterious circum-stances in 1924. They had been used to store some of the treasures of the imperial collection, and Reginald Johnston, worried that the eunuchs were disposing of palace treasures, had just organized an inventory. Before he could inspect

An 18th-century celadon jar modelled on a Bronze Age form. Its archaism is further emphasized by the elegant crackle in the glaze which recalls Guan ware of the Song dynasty. Collecting such pieces with antiquarian associations demonstrated an emperor's knowledge and taste.

the contents of the Palace for Establishing Happiness, it caught fire. Neighbouring buildings were threatened and:

had it not been for the timely arrival of a fire-engine sent by the Italian Legation it is possible that the emperor's own palace, and that of the empress, which were not far off, might also have been reduced to ashes. I found the emperor and the empress standing on a heap of charred wood, sadly contemplating the spectacle. Several of the princes had already arrived and officers of the Neiwufu [Imperial Household Department] were fussily doing their best to instruct the well-disciplined Italian firemen in the art of how not to extinguish fires.

Johnston also encountered Mr Gascoigne and Mr and Mrs Carlson of the British Legation, all in evening dress covered in smuts. They had seen the fire from the roof of the nearby Grand Hotel de Pékin and had got into the Forbidden City by mingling with the Italian firemen. Johnston presented them to the emperor, who thanked them for helping put out the fire, though it is equally possible that they were hoping to help themselves to imperial treasures.[97]

The last great garden to be built within the walls of the Forbidden City was that constructed in a narrow space running northwards from the Palace of Tranquil Longevity in the northeast corner of the Forbidden City. It was built for the Qianlong emperor between 1771 and 1776, for his proposed retirement. It consists of a string of four courtyards, each with its own character, each concealed from the next. In the first courtyard is a fine old catalpa tree, which antedated the construction of the garden but was carefully incorporated in the design, its beautiful clusters of pink flowers give their name to the open-sided lodge at the centre, the Pavilion of Ancient Flowers.

On one side is the Pavilion of the Ceremony of Purification with a 'cup-floating stream', one of four in the Forbidden City. Curving grooves with a hidden outlet are cut into the stone floor. Water was drawn from a well and stored in great vats before being poured into the meandering stream, and little cups of wine were floated along on the water. Cup-floating streams were made for a drinking game which commemorated a famous party given in 353 by Wang Xizhi (303–61), the great calligrapher whose works were amongst the 'Three Rarities' prized by the Qianlong emperor.[98] Little cups of wine were floated past his guests, who had to compose a line of poetry when a cup floated by, or pay the forfeit of drinking the wine.[99]

The closely packed, rock-filled gardens within the inner palace had charm compared with the solemn splendour of the outer palace, but the series of lakes to the west of the Forbidden City (outside the walls but still 'forbidden' to all but honoured guests) must have offered far greater relief from the strictures of palace life, and cooler air. There were three lakes, known as 'seas': the Beihai (North Sea), Zhonghai (Central Sea), and Nanhai (Southern Sea). Dug in the twelfth century, they were divided by bridges and improved by Qubilai Khan, the Yongle emperor and the Qing emperors, who used the Sea Palaces as an extension of the Forbidden City.

The Beihai is the largest lake, with the Round Fortress, or Round Town, at its southern tip. The Round Fortress was built from earth excavated during works on the lake during the Mongol Yuan dynasty (1279–1368). Here, the Guangxu emperor received the diplomatic credentials of Mr O'Connor, the British Minister, in 1893,[100] and Cao Kun, President of the Chinese Republic, was imprisoned in the Round Fortress by the warlord Feng Yuxiang in 1924 during the *coup d'état* watched by Puyi from the terrace in the Imperial Garden. The nearby island, known as Hortensia Island during the Yuan and Ming, was renamed White Dagoba island in 1651 when the great white stupa was built there to commemorate the first visit of a Dalai Lama to Beijing.[101] The *dagoba* is a Buddhist stupa (a building intended to house Buddhist relics) in the Tibetan style and is the dominant building on the island, which is scattered with pavilions. Its diplomatic use, to convince visiting Tibetan and Mongol lamas of the Qing dynasty's interest in their form of Buddhism, is reinforced by the small building in front, covered in green- and yellow-glazed tiles, which houses a statue of Yamantaka, a fierce deity of Lamaistic (Tibetan and Mongolian) Buddhism with seven heads, thirty-four hands, sixteen feet and a rosary of human skulls.

The 'cup-floating' game so pleased the Qianlong emperor that he had a complex channel made inside the palace. In the Tan zhe temple southwest of the city, where the emperor built a 'travelling palace' so he could stay overnight. The temple is illustrated in Linqing's memoirs, 1847–50.

There are stone inscriptions all over the island inscribed with the calligraphy of the Shunzhi and Yongzheng emperors describing its history, and a hall of great significance is the Tower of Ancient Scripts where more than four hundred stone tablets, inscribed with the calligraphy of Wang Xizhi, his son and nephew, amongst others, were placed at the order of the Qianlong emperor. The Qianlong emperor added his own calligraphy to the island in the form of a four-sided stele. The inscription on the rear (dated 1751) records the rescue of famous stones collected by the Huizong emperor (r. 1101–25) for his imperial garden in Kaifeng. It states that many rocks were transported and placed here 'in fanciful positions to make them look like dragons' scales'.[102]

On the eastern shore of the lake were the Altar of Silkworms and the imperial boathouse where the pleasure boats were stored. On the northeastern shore of the lake is a cluster of Buddhist temples, built during the Qing, and a pretty little garden self-contained behind its walls, the Jingxinzhai or Studio of the Pure Heart. This was first constructed in the Ming, rebuilt in the Qianlong reign as a separate study for the imperial princes and was, later, one of the Empress Dowager Cixi's favourite places in the Sea Palaces. It is an interesting construction, set against the rear wall of the great open lake enclosure of an imperial-sized park, and recalls the smaller, private gardens of the Yangtse delta.

The Middle Sea had its own separate boathouse and a series of buildings on the western shore. To the north is the Ziguangge, the Hall of Polar Brightness (another reference to the Polar star, symbol of the emperors). On the foundations of a terrace where the Ming emperors used to sit and enjoy the view, the first Qing emperor to live in the Forbidden City, the Shunzhi emperor (reigned 1644–61), built the hall to watch military reviews. Towards the end of the Qing, foreign diplomats were received here, in less formal conditions than inside the Forbidden City proper. The first such audience was held in 1873 and began at 9 a.m. rather than the traditional pre-dawn hour that eighteenth century Dutch envoys had had to endure. The Japanese ambassador was received first, and then the Russian ambassador, 'dean' (or senior member) of the diplomatic corps, made a congratulatory speech.[103]

Just south of the Hall of Polar Brightness was the Yiluandian or Hall of Ceremonial Phoenixes, where the Empress Dowager Cixi stayed, and where she died in 1908. An American artist, Katherine Carl, commissioned to paint portraits of Cixi, described her arrival at the Sea Palaces where she was rowed across the lake, with its tall pink lotus flowers, in a houseboat with carpets, tea tables and chairs. 'I lay back amongst the cushions, as we glided swiftly along, past beautiful pavilions, with splendid trees overhanging the lake and lovely flowers growing wherever there was a place to plant them.'[104] She witnessed the empress dowager at work, receiving New Year greetings from the ladies of the diplomatic corps. A few days later, the Lantern Festival (held on the fifteenth day of the first month and marking the end of the New Year celebrations) held in the Sea Palaces.

Tall eunuchs, in gala red, stood around the courts, holding great lanterns aloft, like huge caryatides with luminous burdens. Others with fanciful vermilion lanterns wound in and out through corridors and courts . . . they manoeuvred and made intricate designs and luminous tableaux, holding aloft their red-globed lanterns to form characters and phrases of 'felicitous omen' . . . After the torch- and lantern-lit processions, and the glowing tableaux, a pair of illuminated dragons writhed into the courtyard and struggled for the flaming pearl which flitted around with elusive fantastic movements, ever beyond their grasp.

For a fortnight after the Lantern Festival, there were fireworks every evening on the banks of the lake. Wrapped in fur rugs and wearing fur-lined robes, the emperor, Cixi and the palace ladies were pushed in ice sledges across the lake, accompanied by eunuchs carrying horn lanterns as the fireworks were let off.

There were beautiful set-pieces, pagodas, with ladies on balconies, pavilions with grapevines, wisteria arbours, and beds of flowers so lifelike they seemed to grow at the side of the luminous cascades, and many other effects I had never before seen in my life.

One day there were daylight fireworks which scattered 'all sorts of curious paper devices . . . fish dragons and animals'.[105]

The southernmost lake, the Southern Sea, forms round a small island, the Yingtai or Ocean Terrace, used by the Liao and Jin rulers of Beijing in the twelfth century as a stage. In 1898, the dowager empress imprisoned the Guangxu emperor (r. 1875–1908) on this island for two years. After two humiliating defeats by European forces in the Opium Wars (1840–42, 1860) and the Japanese in 1894, many were deeply worried about China's inability to resist such incursions. The Guangxu emperor supported a reform movement led by Kang Youwei (1858–1927), publishing a series of decrees supporting the introduction of scientific studies, the abolition of the old-fashioned 'eight-legged essays' in the official examination system, the adoption of Western military drill and methods, the foundation of a modern university in Beijing and the abolition of sinecures. There was considerable opposition from those whose positions were founded on the old, traditional forms, and the dowager empress took action. She became regent once again, Kang Youwei fled to Hong Kong, six of his supporters were executed and many others removed from office. The Guangxu emperor remained a prisoner on his island until both he and Cixi were forced to flee the capital in 1900 as foreign troops marched in to destroy the Boxer rebellion and rescue the foreign diplomats and residents besieged nearby in the Legation Quarter.

Temples and shrines

W ithin the Forbidden City there were over fifteen shrines or altars, and in the Sea Palaces at least another seven. The majority were Buddhist halls but there were also several places where Taoist observances took place, two Confucian shrines and a Silkworm Altar.

The shrines and halls within the Forbidden City allowed the emperor and his family to carry out the sort of rituals that might be practised by other wealthy families, showing reverence to Confucius, the source of family ritual; to Taoism, another important facet of Chinese belief often associated with the search for health and avoidance of bad luck and, Buddhism, the only popular faith in China which offered a fairly positive view of the afterlife with its western paradise. Some emperors personally favoured Taoism, others Buddhism, but all observed traditional rituals for fear of angering the gods if they failed to feed and worship them.

The emperor's ritual observances were seen as essential to the well-being of the state. As the mediator between heaven and earth, his observances served to maintain the relationship between the two. Though it was mainly through his administration that he preserved the well-being of his people, there were certain ritual actions that demonstrated his care for them and his position as their leader. There was a distinction between 'official' ritual sites, where the emperor made public sacrifices, and private ones within the confines of the Forbidden City. The Ministry of Rites maintained the public altars and temples, with the help of labourers working out their tax dues, and the ritual regulations for each dynasty decreed the times and types of rituals.

The Imperial Ancestral Temple lay to the southeast of the Meridian Gate (it is now known as the Worker's Cultural Palace). The temple was established by the Yongle emperor and used throughout the Ming and Qing. The imperial ancestors were worshipped here at each of the four seasons, on New Year's Day and on the emperor's birthday. There were also sets of imperial ancestral tablets in the 'first rank state altars' (of Heaven, Earth and Agriculture)[106] and, for private rituals, in the Hall for Worshipping Ancestors in the southern part of the Six Eastern Palaces. This was first built during the Ming and renovated at least four times during the Qing. Here, the emperor or a representative would make

Imperial ancestral portraits displayed for the New Year. Ancestral portraits were intimate things made for the family and not for outsiders, who were forbidden to know what the emperor looked like. Ancestral worship, the centre of family worship for the Chinese, was also followed by the Qing emperors.

special offerings on the imperial birthday, at the winter solstice and on the first day of the New Year, the three 'great festivals'.

Parallel to the Imperial Ancestral Temple, to the west, is the Altar to the Earth and Grain (now part of the Sun Yat-sen Park), with a great square white marble platform spread with different coloured earths, in front of the Hall of Prayer. The coloured earth represented the five directions: west, white; east, green; north, black; south, red; centre, yellow; and the association of earth and grain symbolized the dominion of the emperor and its harvests, for whose success he prayed. The emperor made twice-yearly sacrifices here, in spring praying for a good harvest and in autumn giving thanks. During the Qing, special extra sacrifices were made in the case of drought, when the emperor would pray for rain; though during the disastrous floods in the Beijing area in 1801, the Jiaqing emperor came to pray for dry weather.[107]

The emperor's involvement with the agricultural year was also seen in observances at other imperial temples surrounding the Forbidden City. The Ming emperors established altars to the sun, moon and earth in the eastern, western and northern suburbs respectively, and larger altars to agriculture and heaven to the south of the Forbidden City. For many Ming emperors, the annual ritual visits to these altars were the only times they left the Forbidden City. They went to the Altar to the Sun in the spring, to the Altar to the Moon in the autumn, to the Altar to the Earth at the summer solstice, and to the two great southern altars at the New Year and winter solstice.

Before any of the major sacrifices at these imperial altars, emperors abstained from eating meat, onions, garlic and spicy foods, drinking alcohol, listening to music, and from sexual relations for three days. During the Qing, there was a special building in the Forbidden City, the Hall of Abstinence, where the emperor stayed to prepare himself (and there was another Hall of Abstinence in the Temple of Heaven for his overnight stay at the winter solstice). Though there were slight changes in the rituals over the centuries, in principle the great imperial procession to the Temple of Heaven at the winter solstice was made to report to heaven on the events of the past year and to offer prayers and sacrifices to heaven for favour in the coming year. During the Qing, the imperial ancestors were invited to participate in this important ritual. On entering the Temple of Heaven the emperor descended from his elephant-drawn chariot and went to the smaller of the blue-roofed circular halls, where he offered incense and prayed to the ancestral tablets kept there. After a night spent in fasting and meditation, he dressed in plum silk robes and went to the terraced altar where animals were prepared for sacrifices. The imperial ancestral tablets were brought out to participate in the offering to heaven of slaughtered animals, bolts of silk and much incense. In the first month after the winter solstice, the emperor returned to the Temple of Heaven to pray for a good agricultural year.

Just to the west of the semicircular enclosure of the Temple of Heaven was another imperial altar, known in the Ming as the Altar to Mountains and Rivers. In the Qing, it was rebuilt as the Altar to Agriculture, where the emperor would come every spring to plough a small patch of land and sow rice. The officials who accompanied him also ploughed and sowed four varieties of millet. The emperor's plough and trowel were yellow, and the oxen that pulled the plough were also yellow, with yellow harnesses. As the emperor ploughed his eight furrows, the Minister of Finance followed, wielding a whip, with the Viceroy of the Metropolitan Province carrying the box of rice. Lesser officials ploughed eighteen furrows and 'finally some aged peasants finished the work'. The grain produced by these high-grade agriculturalists was kept in a special granary and could only be used for sacrifices.[108]

Just inside the East Glorious Gate of the Forbidden City is a large complex, the Hall of Literary Glory. On the western side of the first courtyard is the Hall for the Transmission of the Mind, built in 1685, which held 'ancestral tablets' of many of the gods of the Chinese tradition. These included the legendary emperors Fu Xi (said to have invented hunting, fishing, herding, cooking and making musical instruments), Shen Nong (inventor of agriculture, the medicinal qualities of plants and the system of barter), the Great Yu (another mythical emperor, credited with taming floods) and Confucius. The emperor came here every year in the eighth month and made offerings in the hall. A portrait of Confucius and another group of Confucian 'ancestral tablets' formed a shrine, kept next to the Imperial Study just inside the Gate of Heavenly Purity. This was visited every New Year's Day by the emperor, who kowtowed to Confucius as part of his ceremonial round.

The main Taoist building in the Forbidden City was the Hall of Imperial Peace in the centre of the Imperial Garden, constructed during the Ming. The Temple of the Four Gods and the Hall of the Treasures of the Sky to the east of the six East Palaces, were Ming Taoist shrines. Though the Qing emperors

included lighting incense at Taoist altars in their New Year's Day rituals, the most famous imperial Taoist was the Ming emperor Jiajing (r. 1522–67). After the attempt on his life, he retreated to the Sea Palaces, where he held Taoist rituals involving ambergris and pearls, special incense and several thousand ounces of gold dust. Some of the rituals lasted twelve days and nights.[109] Whilst not following the excessive interest of the Jiajing emperor, the Qianlong emperor had Taoist priests chant for him on his birthday and the following thirty-five days.

The death of the Yongle emperor's wife was commemorated with Buddhist sacrificial ceremonies[110]. The emperor also presided over the publication of Buddhist texts and actively stressed the significance of Buddhism in bringing minority tribes on the southwestern borders into the Chinese fold.[111]

It was in the Qing that Lamaist Buddhism, as practised in Mongolia and Tibet, became 'the official religion of the country'.[112] In the pre-conquest period Lamas from the *Sa-skya-pa* sect were influential amongst the Jin, and their popularity continued, particularly because their form of Buddhism 'promised heavenly favour – and earthly legitimacy – to the monarch who became their patron'.[113] The Ming and early Qing saw a series of measures designed to contain the enduring Mongol threat and diplomatic measures to bring the Lamaist Tibetans under Chinese control, played an important part. One Buddhist tenet was that of the *cakravartin* or 'world ruler', a concept embraced in the sixth century by Emperor Wu of the Liang dynasty, to which subsequent Chinese emperors also subscribed. This was developed in Tibetan Buddhism in the creation of lineages of reincarnation. The Qing emperors' enthusiastic adoption

The traditional Chinese calendar was issued officially and as the emperor was the summit of official power, he personally inaugurated the agricultural year by ploughing a ceremonial furrow after the winter solstice.

of these ideas can be seen in the *thangka* of the Qianlong emperor as a reincarnation of the Bodhisattva Mañjuśri. favoured by the Mongols who made annual pilgrimages to the Wutai mountains in North China, supposedly the abode of Mañjuśri.[125]

In the Buddhist halls of the Forbidden City, many Lamaist traces can be seen. In the Buddhist Building, at the very back of the Palace of Tranquil Longevity, there is a cabinet with an upper screen containing sixty-five images of the Buddha in various poses, interspersed with figures of the Dalai Lamas (recognizable by their pointed hats), while the murals in the same building depict Lamaist groupings with many-armed figures. The three-storey Pavilion of the Rain of Flowers on the opposite side of the Forbidden City contains a circular altar in the Lamaist style, with a white marble base and figures of mother-of-pearl, blue enamel and bronze. In front of the Hall of Exuberance (in the northwestern corner of the Forbidden City, where the Buddhas of the western paradise were worshipped) a Bodhi tree (*Ficus religiosa*) was planted. Said to be the type of tree under which the Buddha achieved enlightenment, it provided seeds, which were made into Buddhist rosaries, and leaves, which were cut into a perfect upside-down heart shape, on which court artists painted Buddhist scenes, the medium referring back to the religious founder.

The Manchu Qing dynasty introduced one further form of worship into the Forbidden City, the shamanism that was characteristic of Manchu belief and which had nothing to do with the Chinese over whom they ruled. Shamans, common throughout northeastern and inner Asia, interpreted heavenly portents and signs, and were healers. The Qing ancestors had sacrificed white horses to heaven and black oxen to the earth to 'commemorate auspicious events'; they also made sacrifices at spring and autumn and shot arrows into willow leaves, 'the results to be interpreted by the shamans'.[115] They brought their own specific legends, associating Nurhaci (the patron saint of his lineage) with magpies because he was said to have been concealed from his enemies by a flock of magpies.[116] According to Manchu legend a magpie impregnated a heavenly maiden who subsequently gave birth to the founding ancestor.[117] The Manchu Qing emperors worshipped heaven in shamanic rituals in spring and summer, adding a further New Year ritual, perhaps because the New Year was so significant to the Chinese. Daily sacrifices were held in the Palace of Earthly Tranquillity, a hall associated with women, who played an important part in the rituals. A black pig was sacrificed daily, and offered with washed grain. The pig's neck-bone was attached to the top of a 'spirit pole' and some cooked pork and grain were

Though they adapted to many forms of Chinese life, the Manchus of the Qing dynasty retained much of their own heritage. The clothing and hairstyles were different, their taste in food was different, as was their attitude to physical exercise, and they made daily sacrifices of meat to magpies and crows on these tall 'spirit poles'.

placed in an offering plate near the top of the pole, which was raised and placed straight upright. A number of these 'spirit poles', easily accessible to crows and sacred magpies, can be seen in the Forbidden City.

An important duty of the palace kitchens was the preparation of food offerings. Details of the daily offerings at ancestral altars during the reign of the first Ming emperor give an idea of the huge quantity of food offerings made daily or monthly to the many altars within the Forbidden City:

> On the FIRST DAY of each month, rolled fried cakes; on the SECOND DAY, finely granulated sugar; followed by tea from Sichuan, sugared butter biscuits, twice-cooked fish, steamed rolls with steamed mutton, clover honey biscuits, sugared steamed biscuits, pork fryings, sugared jujube cakes, oven baked bread, sugar-filled steamed bread, mutton filled steamed bread, rice-flour cakes, fat-filled pastries, honey cakes, baked puff-pastry, rhomboid-shaped cakes, flaky filled pastries, marrow cakes, rolled biscuits, crisp honey biscuits, scalded dough baked breads, sesame oil noodles, pepper and salt breads, water-reed shoots, sesame and sugar-filled breads, smartweed flowers, soured cream and thousand-layer baked breads.[118]

As well as these specified daily offerings, there were monthly offerings:

> Starting in the FIRST LUNAR MONTH with leeks, fresh greens, clams, perch, chicken and duck eggs. In the SECOND MONTH there was new tea, rapeseed greens, celery and goslings. In the THIRD MONTH, new bamboo shoots, cabbage, carp, chicken and duck eggs; in the FOURTH MONTH: turnips, cherries, loquats, plums, apricots, cucumbers, piglets and pheasants; in the FIFTH MONTH, pumpkins, gourds, aubergines, peaches, plums, wheat and barley grains; in the SIXTH MONTH, lotus seed-pods, watermelons, winter melons, herring; in the SEVENTH MONTH, snow pears, water-lily seeds, jujubes and grapes; in the EIGHTH MONTH, millet, rice, lotus root, taro, ginger shoots, crabs; in the NINTH MONTH, chestnuts, oranges, bream, red beans; in the TENTH MONTH, yams, chrysanthemums, tangerines, hares; in the ELEVENTH MONTH, buckwheat noodles, sugarcane, venison, wild goose, swan, cormorant, quail, partridge and in the TWELFTH MONTH, spinach, mustard greens, silver pomfret and bream.[11]

Ordinary Chinese set great store by preparations for the Chinese New Year. Their rituals for the Kitchen God were echoed in the Forbidden City. The Qing 'Kitchen God' was worshipped in the Palace of Earthly Peace where the stoves for preparing ritual offerings for spirit poles were situated. On the twenty-third day of the twelfth month, sweets were offered to the Kitchen God before he made his annual trip to heaven to report on the household. Since a good report was supposed to bring good luck in the forthcoming year, the offerings were intended to sweeten his tongue. The Qing offered more: a fat sheep, fruits, vegetables, cake, soups, tea and sugar; and it is reported that the Qianlong emperor liked to 'sacrifice to the Kitchen God in person, beating a drum and singing a popular song called (presumably with some irony), "The emperor in search of honest officials"'[120] and lighting fire-crackers to speed the Kitchen God on his way. In the complex rota of offerings and obeisances, both privately within the Forbidden City and publicly outside, it is pleasant to think that the Qianlong emperor actually enjoyed this particular more domestic and light-hearted offering.

It was the Qianlong emperor's wife, the Empress Xiaoxian (who died in 1738) who promoted the cult of silkworms within the court. Though imperial women were significant in the shamanistic cult within the palace, the cult of silkworms was a new one, celebrated at the Beihai, (Northern Lake) in the Western or Sea Palaces. The empresses and palace ladies kept silkworms in specially built sheds on the east side of the lake where there was also an Altar to the Silkworms. Sacrifices were offered by the women to the Goddess of Silkworms on an auspicious day in the third month, and the women also held imperial inspections of the mulberry leaves before they were offered to the imperial silkworms. In this ritual, the palace women and the empresses reflected the love of silkworms felt by many Chinese children who reared silkworms themselves.[121]

Entertaining the emperors

ive well-preserved stages still exist in the Forbidden City. The major stage in the Forbidden City is the Pavilion of Pleasant Sounds, which is behind the Palace of Tranquil Longevity in the northeast corner of the enclosure. It was built in 1772 and twice renovated in the nineteenth century. It is a tapering, three-storey building raised on a high stone platform which projects out into the courtyard. All round the courtyard are galleries, and opposite the stage is a two-storey building, the 'imperial box'. The best seat was a couch surrounded by screens, in the main bay of the ground floor. The glass doors would be folded back, unless it was very cold, in which case the stage could be viewed through the glass.

The main stage is on the lowest floor with two smaller stages above it, so that elaborate representations, for example of earth and heaven, could be staged at the same time. There were openings to allow actors access to one stage from the other, and pulley systems to hoist them up and down. Scenery was stored in pits below the stage, to be hauled into place when needed.

Dramatic performances were held at New Year and on the imperial birthday. When the Dowager Empress Cixi celebrated her fiftieth birthday, in 1885, marathon theatrical performances, six or seven hours long, were put on every day for eight consecutive days in the ninth month, and then for a further nine days in the tenth month, with simultaneous performances in the smaller theatre in the courtyard of the Palace of Eternal Spring. The actors (all men) wore fantastically elaborate costumes, larger than life versions of court dress, religious robes or military costumes, all made of silks and heavily embroidered. The performances, a mixture of speech and song, were of well-known stories, often with a religious theme – 'The Arhats Crossing the Sea' or 'The Golden Lotus Springing from the Earth' – and the audience would come and go, or eat and drink whilst watching, always able to pick up the thread of the drama.

Princess Der Ling described Cixi's attendance at a religious play entitled: 'The Empress of Heaven's Party or Feast to all the Buddhist Priests to eat her famous peaches and drink her best wine.' Cixi attended with her favourite brown dog, Sea Otter; 'A more homely dog I never saw. It had nothing to recommend it in any way', said Der Ling.[122] Seated opposite the stage, the glass doors thrown open, Cixi would watch, sometimes taking her siesta in the room behind whilst the play went on. The play opened with an actor, dressed in yellow and red as a Buddhist priest, descending from heaven on a cotton-wool cloud, 'suspended in the air and apparently floating'. As he floated down, five pagodas rose from below the stage.[123] The next scene was a comedy in which a monkey consumed the Empress of Heaven's feast of peaches and wine. Later scenes included slapstick with the monkey becoming drunk and battles between troupes of monkeys and imperial guards.[124]

In the Studio of Fresh Fragrance, in the northwest of the Forbidden City, there were two stages, an open pavilion in the courtyard and a tiny interior stage behind, not for bad weather but for different types of performance during family banquets. These were both renovated by the Qianlong emperor, who received congratulations from his high officials and held banquets here with theatrical entertainments on the open stage.

The most curious stage in the Forbidden City is the tiny one in the Study of Peaceful Old Age. Like the interior stage in the Studio of Fresh Fragrance, it is a building within a building, a small pavilion raised slightly above the floor, with a tiled roof topped with a large gold boss. The building-within-a-building effect is enhanced by the complex *trompe l'oeil* painting of the surrounding walls and ceiling. The walls are painted with bamboo lattice fences, pine trees and palace buildings with red columns and yellow roofs. The garden effect of the bamboo fences is enhanced by the bamboo arbour with trailing wisteria flowers which is painted over the ceiling. The effect is of an elegant but rustic tea-house, and on the little stage eunuchs performed 'tea plays' of the sort that ordinary people in Beijing would have enjoyed in the public tea-houses.[125]

The Ming emperors were not known for their love of sport, going to the Sea Palaces for the views, whilst the Manchus used the area more actively. The Kangxi emperor recalled his upbringing in terms of hunting: 'Since my childhood, with either gun or bow, I have killed in the wild 135 tigers and 20 bear, 25 leopards, 20 lynx, 14 tailed *mi* deer, 96 wolves, and 132 wild boar as well as countless ordinary stags and deer.' For Kangxi and other Manchus, hunting was 'a skill that eludes words . . . The hunt is also a training for war, a test of discipline and organization.'[126]

The Qianlong emperor had stelae engraved with his great grandfather's 1636 complaint about urbanized young Manchus set up near the Arrow Pavilion and at the imperial drill grounds, to encourage the study of the traditional customs of the Manchus.[127] Tutors were appointed for the imperial princes, to teach them Manchu, Mongolian and archery, and imperial nobles were periodically examined in Manchu, riding and archery. Such examinations took place in the Forbidden City on the great open space surrounding the Archery Pavilion. Apart from the examinations, this was a place where the emperors and their sons could practise riding and archery. Military displays and archery and Mongolian wrestling exhibitions were also held on the western shore of the Middle Sea.

The emperors' horses were painted by the Jesuit artists Jean-Denis Attiret and Giuseppe Castiglione. Castiglione and Attiret also painted portraits of the imperial hunting dogs, lean whippet-like animals. One of Attiret's albums, still in the Forbidden City, shows ten horses painted in the Western style, white, dappled grey, chestnut and palomino, all named (in Manchu) and standing in Chinese landscapes.

The Dowager Empress Cixi kept a lot of smaller dogs – Pekinese and other types. The American artist Katherine Carl was more taken with Sea Otter than Princess Der Ling, describing him as a sort of Skye terrier, 'most intelligent and clever at tricks. Among other tricks, he will lie down as dead at Her Majesty's command, and never move until she tells him to, no matter how many others may speak to him.' Her other favourite dog, a fawn Pekinese, was beautiful but untrained and she gave him the name *Shadza* (fool). Miss Carl was very fond of dogs, making daily visits to the 'kennels', and eventually received a Pekinese as a present from Cixi. She noted, 'the dogs at the Palace are kept in a beautiful pavilion with marble floors. They have silken cushions to sleep on, and special eunuchs to attend to them. They are taken for daily outside exercise and given their baths with regularity. There are hundreds of dogs in the Palace, the young Empress, the Princesses and Ladies, and even the eunuchs, having their own.' Cixi hated cats but some of the eunuchs kept them, well out of her way.

The Ming emperors kept cats: the Yongle emperor used to give palace-bred cats as presents, and amongst the surviving paintings thought to be by the Xuande emperor (r. 1426–35) is a handscroll of five kittens in a garden.[128]

Skating and kite-flying were amongst the entertainments offered in the Western Garden. The numerous boathouses in the Western Garden contained houseboats that could convey the imperial family across the water or into the

The martial Qianlong emperor was proud of his 'ten great victories' including campaigns in Burma and against the Gurkhas. They were commemorated in copperplate engravings made in Paris and based on drawings by the Jesuit fathers Castiglione, Sichelbarth, Attiret and Salusti. Here the army victorious in East Turkestan is shown in camp. Paris, 1774.

middle of the lakes to watch firework displays on the shores. They also housed the sledges that were used instead of boats in the winter. Great skating displays were held on the three 'seas' during the winter, partly as entertainment, partly as a demonstration of martial skill. There are several paintings in the imperial collections depicting skating events, including one by Yao Wenhuan of a New Year banquet in 1761, held in the open air. The lake is frozen solid; two sledges, one flying the imperial standard, are parked by a clump of bare trees. The emperor is seated in the open-fronted Hall of Polar Brightness, with many of his guests out in the open or under canopies, in a temperature that would typically be minus five degrees centigrade. Even with the special palace chafing dishes, filled with boiling water, the food must have cooled quickly. Out on the lake, which was specially smoothed with heated flat irons to prevent accidents, soldiers, some with banners fixed on their backs, skate in a series of circles, some shooting arrows at targets fixed on a red-painted frame set up on the ice.[129]

In the spring, winds often blow in Beijing, and April was the month when kites were brought out in the Sea Palaces. Katherine Carl was summoned by the dowager empress to watch. 'The kites were of paper, wonderfully fashioned, representing birds, fish, bats, and even personages. The strings were wound on curiously-shaped reels and the cleverness with which Her Majesty let out the string and manipulated the kites was wonderful.'[130]

7

Collecting and consuming

In the newly built Forbidden City, all that the Ming imperial family needed was supplied by the eunuch departments. But for some emperors, with an interest in Chinese culture and a taste for the antique, this was not enough. Within the palace were some treasures rescued from the Song imperial palace by the Mongols; these and further items collected during the Yuan were stamped with the Ming imperial seal and formed the basis of the imperial collections, to which subsequent emperors added.[131] The Yongle emperor invited painters to the court, to decorate the new hall and to paint his portrait and make bird, flower or landscape paintings for the imperial collection. He also invited calligraphers (whose art was more highly esteemed than pictorial painting) to work in the Hall of Literary Profundity in the southeastern corner of the Forbidden City. A number of painters stayed in the Forbidden City for some years, and some were offered official titles. During the reign of the Xuande emperor, a painting academy was established in the Forbidden City. The emperor held examinations for prospective painters, awarding Zhou Wenjing first prize in the category 'old trees and wintry birds'.[132] He was himself fond of painting , specializing in painting animals from the imperial stables: dogs, cats, monkeys, goats and birds.[133]

The blue and white porcelains of the Xuande emperor's reign are particularly esteemed but, as they were produced thousands of miles away at the imperial kilns in Jingdezhen, by anonymous craftsmen, it is unlikely that he influenced the designs in any way. He may have had more influence on bronze design; incense burners, altar pieces and smaller bronzes were produced for use within the Forbidden City and are characteristically smooth and elegant in design, often gold-flecked. The emperor's interest in bronzes can be seen from the catalogue produced under his auspices, which still survives.[134]

During the Ming, underglaze blue painting on porcelain was perfected, to become one of the world's most influential wares. An elegant stem-cup of the Xuande reign period (1426–35) depicts horses, reserved in white against a ground of blue waves.

In the early Ming, the cobalt blue used in porcelain decoration was difficult to control and expensive. It was often used sparingly, as in this dish decorated with a dragon and acquatic plants. The dragon has five claws, a design supposedly restricted to imperial use.

A great monument to collecting and scholarship was produced in the Yongle period. Imperial libraries were frequently destroyed by fire, and the Yongle emperor was not the only one to wish to preserve literary works. In 1403 a manuscript compilation, arranged by subject, of all known literature was commissioned. The *Great Encyclopaedia of Yongle* was completed in 1408, comprizing 22,877 *juan* or sections.[135]

The greatest collector in the Forbidden City was the Qianlong emperor. He spent every afternoon in cultural pursuits: writing poetry (42,000 poems are attributed to him, so he must have been busy), practising painting and calligraphy and inspecting the contents of the palace collections. He wrote many inscriptions on ancient paintings, not always to their improvement, but added greatly to the collections of painting, ancient bronzes and jades, which were stored in special boxes and had carved wooden stands for display.[136] He was a patron of the arts, supporting a number of painters at court. The eunuch craft departments of the Ming were replaced by a series of workshops, some staffed by Jesuits, making and repairing clocks, producing glass snuff-bottles with chemicals imported from Europe,[137] carving ivory and jade, making cloisonné enamel and also decorating plain white porcelains shipped from Jingdezhen for decoration within the Forbidden City in brightly coloured enamels. The Jesuit painters who worked for the Qianlong emperor, most notably Giuseppe Castiglione, created a new style of painting, combining Western and Chinese techniques.

The Qianlong emperor extended the imperial collection of antiquities and made sure that his contribution did not go unnoticed. A Neolithic jade disc, thousands of years old, was an important addition to the collection, and is inscribed in the Qianlong emperor's own hand.

Castiglione's major innovation was the introduction of Western portrait painting, using solid colour for the face and robes. To the Chinese, dark shadows on the face suggested evil (as in opera make-up for villains), so Castiglione modified his painting style, avoiding shadowing as far as possible.[138] The Chinese generally avoided portraiture since, as Princess Der Ling explained, 'a portrait is only painted after death, in memorium of the deceased, in order that the following generations may worship the deceased'[139] but the Qianlong emperor, perhaps because the Manchus did not have the same superstition and because he was enthusiastic about the portraiture skills of Castiglione, had many portraits painted of himself. He was depicted in armour on horseback; as the Bodhisattva Mañjuśri; riding a white horse over a white marble bridge with a Western pocket-watch hanging from his belt; wearing Ming-style Chinese clothing and padded shoes; with his family celebrating New Year, and participating in dozens of official events from imperial banquets to inspections of the banner troops and tours of inspection of the south of China.[140]

Elaborate vessels from Western Zhou tombs (*c*. 1000–901 BC) were added to the imperial collection, particularly by the Qianlong emperor. Objects such as this food vessel, decorated with plumed birds, influenced contemporary porcelain production (see p. 47).

Like the Yongle emperor, the Qianlong emperor also ordered in 1772 a massive compilation of existing literature, the *Complete Library of the Four Treasuries*, in which copies of complete texts would be made. First, books had to be collected from all over China: some 10,230 were examined and 3,450 selected for copying. Four sets were made in the first instance, each of 36,000 *juan*, and they were stored in specially built halls including the Hall of the Source of Literature behind the imperial printing house (Hall of Military Eminence) in the southeastern part of the Forbidden City. In the Hall of Military Eminence imperially commissioned works were printed, including in 1728 a massive (10,000 *juan*) encyclopaedia of quotations illustrated with engravings. Though most of the work of the Hall was printed in the traditional way using wood-blocks, the *Complete Library* was produced using a quarter of a million pieces of metal type, which were subsequently melted down for coinage.[141] An unfortunate aspect of the compilation of the *Complete Library* was the Qianlong emperor's pursuit of seditious works, carrying out a massive 'literary inquisition' under the guise of preserving literature.[142]

By the nineteenth century the Forbidden City, its store-rooms already stuffed with treasures and its halls embellished with traditional and Jesuit decorations, saw some changes in style. Where Qianlong had admired the accurate portraiture of the Jesuits, Cixi ordered Der Ling's brother to photograph her in a variety of poses and groups (see pages 33 and 42). She took an interest in the process and 'commanded one of the eunuchs to stand in front of the camera so that she might look through the focusing glass, to see what it was like. Her Majesty exclaimed: "Why is it your head is upside down? Are you standing on your head or your feet?" So we explained when the photograph was taken it would not look that way.'[143]

8

From palace to museum

The Mongols had been driven from the Forbidden City by the Ming in 1368, and in 1644, as Li Zicheng's rebel forces entered, the last Ming emperor fled to Coal Hill, behind the Forbidden City, where he hanged himself from a tree. In the nineteenth century, Western intrusion forced the Qing emperors out of the Forbidden City several times. In September 1860, as Western forces approached Beijing after the second Opium War, the Xianfeng emperor, his consort Cixi and their four-year old son fled to one of their summer palaces, the 'Mountain Village where you can escape the heat' northeast of Beijing. The humiliated emperor never returned to the Forbidden City, and died a year later in his summer palace.

Cixi was forced to flee again in 1900, with the Guangxu emperor, when Western troops entered Beijing to relieve the siege of the Legation (or diplomatic) quarter. For the past few years, rebel bands of 'Boxers' (who practised martial arts) had been concentrating attacks on foreigners and foreign imports like railways. Though they had banded together as a result of extreme poverty caused by poor harvests and drought, and originally used the slogan 'Defeat the Qing' amongst others, they gradually focused on foreigners and gained support from some local officials for their murders of missionaries. There was even considerable support at court for the idea of throwing foreigners out of China, and parts of the imperial army joined them in besieging the diplomatic quarter.[144] As a massed army of British, French, American, Japanese, Russian, Italian, German and Austrian troops marched from Tianjin to Beijing, Cixi slipped out of the Forbidden City to Xi'an. She took the Guangxu emperor with her, from his island prison in the Sea Palaces, probably because she feared that she might lose power if he stayed behind. One of his consorts, 'the Pearl Concubine', is said to have suggested he stay behind, for which defiance she was thrown down a well at the back of the Forbidden City.[145]

The Forbidden City was occupied by foreign troops who looted it freely, and they were joined in looting by foreign residents of Beijing.[146] In October 1901, with permission from the foreign armies still occupying Beijing, Cixi began the long journey back, carried in a yellow sedan chair, sitting in a dragon barge to

cross rivers and making her first railway journey in a Belgian train, fitted with yellow silk and two imperial thrones, on the last few miles into Beijing.

On her return, Cixi opened up the once Forbidden City, inviting diplomatic wives, tourists and missionaries to receptions and parties in the once private palace. In 1908, the Guangxu emperor and Cixi died within a day of each other and the young Henry Aisin Gioro Puyi became the tenth and last emperor of the Qing. Puyi abdicated in 1912, in favour of a republican government, but he was allowed to stay on in the inner palaces of the Forbidden City, whilst the outer halls were opened to the public as a museum. Puyi was interested in Western fashions, favouring pink spats and tweeds, introducing the telephone to the Forbidden City, constructing a tennis court, and acquiring a car.[147] In 1924, the warlord Feng Yuxiang drove him out of the Forbidden City for the last time.

Notes

1. Michael Dillon, *China: a cultural and historical dictionary*, London, Curzon, 1998, p. 104 and related entries.
2. Yu Zhuoyun and Graham Hutt, *Palaces of the Forbidden City*, Harmondsworth, Viking, 1984, p. 27.
3. On the Khitan, see Valerie Hansen, *The Open Empire: a history of China to 1600*, New York, Norton, 2000, pp. 299-307.
4. Ibid., pp. 315-31.
5. Liu Xujie in Fu Xinian *et al.*, translated by Nancy S. Steinhardt, *Chinese Architecture*, New Haven, Yale University Press, 2002, p. 22.
6. Ibid., p. 24.
7. Edward L. Farmer, *Early Ming Government: the evolution of dual capitals*, Cambridge, Massachusetts, Harvard University Press, 1976, p. 43.
8. Shih-shan Henry Tsai, *The Eunuchs in the Ming Dynasty*, New York, State History of New York Press, 1996, p. 34, and Shih-shan Henry Tsai, *Perpetual Happiness: the Ming emperor Yongle*, Seattle, University of Washington Press, 2001, p. 125.
9. Yu and Hutt (see note 2), p. 20.
10. L.C. Goodrich and Chaoyang Fang, *Dictionary of Ming Biography 1368-1644*, New York, Columbia University Press, 1976, p. 1484.
11. Tsai, 2001 (see note 8), p. 126.
12. Yu and Hutt (see note 2), p. 23.
13. Ibid., pp. 21-2.
14. Ibid., pp. 266-79.
15. Liu Lu, 'The Forbidden City during the Qianlong reign' in Zhang Hongxing, *The Qianlong Emperor: Treasures from the Forbidden City*, Edinburgh, National Museums of Scotland, 2002, pp. 151-5.
16. Chronology by Zheng Lianzhang in Yu and Hutt (see note 2), pp. 325-7.
17. E.O. Reischauer and J.K. Fairbank, *East Asia: the Great Tradition*, Boston, Houghton Mifflin, 1960, pp. 304-5.
18. For the individual works see the entries in Dillon (see note 1).
19. L.C. Goodrich, *The Literary Inquisition of Ch'ienlung* [1935], New York, Paragon Reprint, 1966, p. 80, and Reischauer and Fairbank (see note 17), p. 306.
20. Goodrich and Fang (see note 10), p. 328.
21. Ibid., p. 378.
22. Taisuke Mitamura, *Chinese Eunuchs: the structure of intimate politics*, Rutland, Tuttle, 1970, pp. 29-34.
23. Ibid., pp. 36-40.
24. Robert B. Crawford, 'Eunuch Power in the Ming Dynasty' in *T'oung Pao*, vol. LXIX, 3, Leiden, Brill, 1961, p. 118.
25. Ibid., p. 119.
26. Tsai, 1996 (see note 8), p. 21.
27. Ibid., p. 46.
28. Frederick W. Mote in Chang Kwan-chih (ed.), *Food in Imperial China: anthropological and historical perspectives*, New Haven, Yale University Press, 1977, p. 212.
29. Ibid., p. 215.
30. Tsai, 1996 (see note 8), p. 46.
31. Ibid., p. 53.
32. Evelyn S. Rawski, *The Last Emperors: a social history of Qing imperial institutions*, Berkeley, University of California Press, 1998, p. 167.
33. Ibid., p. 179.
34. Reginald Johnston, *Twilight in the Forbidden City*, [1934], Hong Kong, Oxford University Press, 1987, p. 210.
35. Ibid., pp. 214-5.
36. Cheng Qinhua, *Tales of the Forbidden City*, Beijing, Foreign Languages Press, 1997, pp. 51-2.
37. Jacques Gernet, *China and the Christian Impact*, Cambridge, Cambridge University Press, 1986, p. 20.
38. Xu Guangqi or Hsu Kuang-ch'i, see Arthur W. Hummel, *Eminent Chinese of the Ch'ing Period 1644-1912*, [1943-4], Taipei, Literature House, 1964, pp. 316-19.
39. Louis Pfister, *Notices Biographiques et Bibliographiques sur les Jesuites de l'ancienne Mission de Chine*, vol. 1, Shanghai, Imprimerie de la Mission Catholique, 1932, p. 164.
40. Goodrich and Fang (see note 10), p. 1154.
41. Rawski (see note 32), pp. 2-3, and Pamela Kyle Crossley, *A Translucent Mirror: history and identity in Qing imperial ideology*, Berkeley, University of California Press, 1999.
42. See J.J.L. Duyvendak, 'The Last Dutch Embassy to the Chinese Court (1794-1795)' in *T'oung Pao*, vol. XXXIV, Leiden, Brill, 1938.
43. Ibid., pp. 53-5.
44. Ibid., pp. 55-6.
45. Ibid., p. 57.
46. Ibid., p. 62.
47. Liu Lu (see note 15), p. 154.
48. W. F. Jenner (transl.), *From Emperor to Citizen*,

the autobiography of Aisin Gioro Pu Yi, Oxford, Oxford University Press, 1987, p. 121.

49. Zhang Hongxing (see note 15), p. 92.

50. Louise Levathes, *When China Ruled the Seas*, New York, Simon and Schuster, 1994, pp. 131-2.

51. Goodrich and Fang (see note 10), pp. 856-9.

52. Frederick W. Mote, 'Yuan and Ming' in K.C. Chang (ed.), *Food in Chinese Culture*, New Haven, Yale University Press, 1977, pp. 220-1.

53. Su Ching, *Court Dishes of China: the imperial cuisine of the Ch'ing dynasty*, Rutland, Tuttle, 1966, pp. 17-19.

54. Princess Der Ling, *Two Years in the Forbidden City*, London, Fisher Unwin, 1912, p. 51.

55. Jonathan Spence, *Emperor of China: self-portrait of K'ang-hsi*, London, Book Club Associates, 1974, p. 97.

55. Jonathan Spence, 'Ch'ing' in K.C. Chang (see note 52), p. 282.

57. Su Ching (see note 53), p. 19.

58. Spence (see note 55), p. 9.

59. Rawski (see note 32), p. 49.

60. Pamela Kyle Crossley, *The Manchus*, Oxford, Blackwell, 1997, p. 76.

61. Carney T. Fisher, 'Smallpox, Salesmen and Sectarians: Ming-Mongol relations in the Jiajing reign (1522-67)' in *Ming Studies*, 25, Spring, 1988, p. 5.

62. Spence (see note 55), p. 18.

63. Hummel (see note 38), p. 301.

64. Bao Hua Hsieh, 'From Charwoman to Empress Dowager: serving-women in the Ming palace' in *Ming Studies*, 42, Fall, 1999, p. 31.

65. Ibid., p. 30.

66. Ibid., pp. 32-3.

67. Ibid., p. 26.

68. Ibid., p. 35.

69. Ibid., p. 58.

70. Er Si, Shang Hongkuei *et al.*, *Inside Stories from the Forbidden City*, Beijing, New World Press, 1986, pp. 21-3.

71. Qinhua (see note 36), p. 50.

72. Hsieh (see note 64), p. 45.

73. Ibid., p. 45.

74. Goodrich and Fang (see note 10), p. 288.

75. James A. Millward, 'A Uyghur Muslin at Qianlong's Court: the meanings of the Fragrant Concubine' in *Journal of Asian Studies*, 53, no. 2, 1994, p. 435.

76. Zhang Hongxing (see note 15), p. 85.

77. Millward (see note 75), pp. 436-7.

78. She was probably about sixteen since Chinese children are considered to be one *sui* (year old) at birth and their age goes up every Spring Festival. Thus a child born in January could be referred to as three *sui* in March of the same year.

79. Liu Guilin, 'The "Virtuous Imperial Concubine" bears a son' in Er Si, Shang Hongkui, 1986, p. 95.

80. Ibid., pp. 95-6.

81. Ibid., p. 97.

82. Princess Der Ling (see note 54).

83. Ibid., pp. 36-41.

84. Norman Kutcher, *Mourning in Late Imperial China: filial piety and the state*, Cambridge, Cambridge University Press, 1999, p. 1.

85. Ann Paludan, *The Imperial Ming Tombs*, London, Yale, 1981, pp. 154-5.

86. Kutcher (see note 84), p. 88.

87. Ibid., pp. 153-70.

88. Quoted in Jan Stuart and Evelyn Rawski, *Worshiping the Ancestors: Chinese commemorative portraits*, Washington, Smithsonian Institution, 2001, p. 279.

89. Yu and Hutt (see note 2), p. 120.

90. Peter Valder, *The Gardens of China*, Glebe, Florilegium, 2002, p. 132.

91. Reginald Johnston (see note 34), pp. 344-5, 347, 352.

92. Yu and Hutt (see note 2), pp. 132-3.

93. Maggie Keswick, *The Chinese Garden*, London, Frances Lincoln, 2003, pp. 63-8.

94. Yu and Hutt (see note 2), pp. 126-7.

95. Reginald Johnston (see note 34), p. 380.

96. Juliet Bredon and Igor Mitrophanow, *The Moon Year* [1927], Hong Kong, Oxford University Press, 1982, pp. 427-8.

97. Reginald Johnston (see note 34), pp. 335-6.

98. Zhang Hongxing (see note 15), p. 92.

99. Frances Wood, *Blue Guide: China*, London, A & C Black, 1992, p. 267.

100. British diplomatic representatives in China were generally styled minister or minister plenipotentiary in the 19th century: the difference between a minister, minister plenipotentiary and ambassador depended upon the level of authority granted by the Foreign Office in the negotiation of treaties.

101. L.C. Arlington and William Lewisohn, *In Search of Old Peking*, Peking, Henri Vetch, 1935, p. 81.

102. Ibid., p. 87, and Maggie Keswick (see note 93), p. 218.

103. Arlington and Lewisohn (see note 101), p. 101.

104. Katherine A. Carl, *With the Empress Dowager of China*, London, Eveleigh Nash, 1906, p. 92.

105. Ibid., pp. 283-6.

106. Stuart and Rawski (see note 88), p. 45.

107. Susan Naquin, *Peking: Temples and City Life 1400-1900*, Berkeley, University of California Press, 2000, p. 649.

108. Arlington and Lewisohn (see note 101), p. 113.

109. Goodrich and Fang (see note 10), p. 318.

110. Ibid., p. 568.

111. Tsai, 2001 (see note 8), pp. 143, 84-5.

112. Yu and Hutt (see note 2), p. 176.

113. Crossley (see note 41), p. 112.

114. Zhang Hongxing (see note 15), pp. 52-3.

115. Crossley (see note 41), p. 32.

116. Ibid., pp. 49, 119.

117. Rawski (see note 32), p. 233.

118. F.W. Mote in Chang Kwang-chih (see note 28), pp. 216-17.

119. Ibid., pp. 217-18.

120. Rawski (see note 32), p. 265.

121. Chiang Yee, *A Chinese Childhood*, London, Methuen, 1940, pp. 217-21.

122. Princess Der Ling (see note 54), p. 26.

123. Ibid., pp. 28-9.

124. Ibid., pp. 30-5. The anticipated story is that known in Arthur Waley's translation as *Monkey*, alternatively the *Journey to the West*, a fictionalized account of a real 6th-century pilgrimage to India in search of Buddhist texts.

125. Naquin (see note 107), p. 637.

126. Jonathan Spence (see note 55), pp. 9, 12-13.

127. Stuart and Rawski (see note 88), p. 44.

128. Goodrich and Fang (see note 10), p. 287. The painting is now in the Metropolitan Museum, New York.

129. *Palast-museum Peking: Schatze aus der Verbotenen-stadt*, Berliner Festspiele, 1985, pp. 150-2; also on the dust-jacket of Crossley (see note 41).

130. Katherine Carl (see note 104), p. 291.

131. Chang Lin-shen, 'Le Musée nationale du palais: histoire d'une collection' in *Trésors du Musée nationale du Palais, Taipei: Memoire d'empire*, Paris, Réunion des musées nationaux, 1998, pp. 5-6.

132. Hou-mei Sung, 'The Formation of the Ming Painting Academy' in *Ming Studies,* 29, Spring, 1990, p. 44.

133. Some paintings attributed to Xuande are held in American collections, see Goodrich and Fang (see note 10), p. 287.

134. Ibid., p. 286.

135. A *juan*, or section, does not necessarily correspond with a volume, although in this case it is quite close. A later copy was made but much of the encyclopaedia was destroyed during the Boxer uprising in 1900 through fire and vandalism. Most surviving *juan* were looted, many by foreigners.

136. See Zhang Hongxing (see note 15), pp. 34-5, 122, and *Trésors du Musée national du Palais, Taipei: Memoire d'Empire* (see note 131).

137. Emily Byrne Curtis, 'Chinese glass and the Vatican records' in *Transactions of the Oriental Ceramic Society,* 57, 1992-3, pp. 49-58.

138. Zhang Hongxing (see note 15), pp. 30-1.

139. Princess Der Ling (see note 54), p. 200.

140. Zhang Hongxing (see note 15), pp. 30-3, 36-7, 50-3, 58-60, 62-5, 68-74, 80-5, and Stuart and Rawski (see note 88), p. 123.

141. Frances Wood, *Chinese Illustration*, London, British Library, 1985, pp. 40-1.

142. L.C. Goodrich (see note 19).

143. Princess Der Ling (see note 54), p. 219.

144. Naquin (see note 107), pp. 680-83.

145. Hummel (see note 38), p. 732.

146. Diana Preston, *The Boxer Rebellion*, London, Walker, 2000, pp. 283-95.

147. Johnston (see note 34).

Note on Romanization and pronunciation

Chinese is written in characters and has no alphabet. Over some 500 years, Europeans have used different systems of spelling out the sounds of Chinese words in our alphabet (Romanization). In 1958, China adopted a system of Romanization known as 'pinyin', which means 'to spell' or 'phoneticize'. From the late 1970s, throughout the non-Chinese world, pinyin has become the most commonly used system of Romanization. For that reason, and because you may see signs in pinyin Romanization in China, I have used pinyin. It is with some regret that I have succumbed to consistency and used the pinyin Beijing (pronounced Bay-jing) for the city that we used to know as Peking. Peking, based on an early French Romanization system where 'k' stood for a 'j' sound, is a place-name with poetic and romantic association, recreating a vision of the past, a remote walled city filled with silk-robed mandarins and women with tiny bound feet. Peking University insists that it is not Beijing University in English but Peking University, and the abbreviation on your airline baggage tag is PEK, not BEI, but apart from these examples, it seems that consistency is generally valued over poetry, so Beijing it is.

There are some rules of pinyin pronunciation that need to be learnt:
c is pronounced ts as in 'its', but is also aspirated.
q is pronounced ch as in 'chick'.
x is hissed, somewhere between ss and sh.
z is pronounced in a similar way to c but without the aspiration.
zh is pronounced j as in 'jungle'.

Vowels are pronounced in slightly different ways according to their position or combinations so it is easier to give examples as they occur in the book:
The Chinese name for the Forbidden City, Zi jin cheng, is pronounced 'Ts jin cherng'.
The name of the third Ming emperor, Yongle, is pronounced 'Yung-ler'.
Zhejiang province is pronounced 'Jerjee-ang'.
The town of Suzhou is pronounced 'Soo-joe'.
Linqing in Shandong province is pronounced 'Lin-ching'.
Taoranting park in Beijing is pronounced 'Tow (as in towel) ran ting'.
Liulichang, the antique shop street of Beijing, is pronounced 'Lee-oh lee chang'.

The *Li Ji*, one of the Confucian classics, is pronounced 'Lee Jee'.
The Qianlong emperor and the Qing dynasty are pronounced 'Chee-en lorng' and 'Ching' respectively; Qianlong's first wife was the Empress Xiaoxian, or 'See-ow see-en'.
The examination grades of *xiucai*, *juren* and *jinshi* are pronounced 'see-oh tsai', 'jew-ren' and 'jin-shr.'
The Xuande emperor is pronounced 'Soo-an der' and other Ming emperors include Hongzhi or 'Hoong jer', Zhengde or 'Jung-der', Tianqi or 'Tee-en-chee', Chenghua or 'Cherng-hwa' and Jiajing or 'Jee-ah jing'. (Wanli is easy).
The great eunuch maritime explorer was Zheng He or 'Jerng Her'.
The first Ming emperor's family name was Zhu Yuanzhang or 'Jew Yoo-an jang'.
The town of Hangzhou is pronounced 'Hang joe'.
Porcelain comes from Jingdezhen in Jiangxi province or 'Jing der jen' in 'Jee-ang see'.
A famous Chinese Christian convert was Xu Guangqi or 'Sue gwang chee'.
The Zhong Hai or Middle Sea is pronounced 'Joong ha-ee' and the Tai miao is 'Tie miao'.
The Baohedian or Hall of Preserving Harmony is pronounced 'Bow her dee en'.
Bu dong, 'I don't understand', is pronounced 'Boo dong'.
Qing (Ching) emperors include Shunzhi or 'Shoe-ern jer', Yongzheng or 'Yoong jerng', Kangxi or 'Kang shee', Jiaqing or 'Jee-ah ching', Tongzhi or 'Toong jer', Guangxu or 'Gwang-sue', and Xuantong, 'Sue-an toong' whose family name was Puyi, pronounced 'Pooh-ee'. The famous dowager empress of the Qing had a name which means 'motherly and auspicious', Cixi, pronounced 'Tser-see'. She ruled with Empress Cian, pronounced 'Tser-an'.
Cixi's summer palace, Yiheyuan, the garden where harmony is nourished, is pronounced 'Ee-her-you-arn'. The military hero Zhuge Liang is pronounced 'Jew-ger lee-ang'.
The President of the Republic of China imprisoned in the Round Town was Cao Kun, pronounced 'Tsao koo-ern'.
The Studio of the Pure Heart, Jingxinzhai, is pronounced 'Jing shin jai'; the Hall of Polar Brightness, Ziguangge, is 'Ts gwang ger', the Hall of Ceremonial Phoenixes or Yiluandian is 'Ee lwan dee-en'.

Chronology

Time	Period
960–1279	Song dynasty.
947–1125	Liao dynasty (North China).
1125–1215	Jin dynasty (North China).
1271–1368	Yuan (Mongol) dynasty.
1368–1644	Ming dynasty.
1644–1911	Qing (Manchu) dynasty.

Time	Events
1368	Ming dynasty, with its capital at Nanjing, established after the overthrow of the Mongols.
1403	Yongle emperor seizes power and decides to move the Ming capital to Beijing.
1406	Orders go out for the provision of timber and other building materials for the Forbidden City.
1417–21	First major construction of Forbidden City.
1421	Fire destroys the three main halls.
1421	2,800 serving women in the Forbidden City killed when suspected of rebellion.
1514	Firework display sets fire to two palace buildings.
1524	Sixteen consorts try to murder the Jiajing emperor.
1531	Corner tower is struck by lightning.
1632	Adam Schall von Bell holds the first mass in the Forbidden City.
1655	The first Dutch embassy is received in the Forbidden City.
1765	Jesuit artist Castiglione paints a *trompe l'oeil* in the Hall of Mental Cultivation.
1771–6	The Qianlong emperor builds the Palace of Tranquil Longevity in the Forbidden City.
1794	Another Dutch embassy is received in the Forbidden City.
1885	Dowager Empress Cixi celebrates her fiftieth birthday in the Forbidden City.
1893	The British Minister presents his credentials in the Forbidden City.
1900	The Forbidden City is occupied by foreign troops after relieving the siege of the Legation quarter in Beijing.
1901	Dowager Empress Cixi returns to the Forbidden City and invites diplomatic wives to tea.
1908	Dowager Empress Cixi dies in the Forbidden City.
1912	The last emperor, Puyi, abdicates but continues to live in the Forbidden City.
1922	Puyi's wedding night in the Forbidden City.
1924	Puyi leaves the Forbidden City.
1925	Forbidden City opened as a public museum.

Further reading

Katherine A. Carl, *With the Empress Dowager of China*, London, Eveleigh Nash, 1906.

Pamela Kyle Crossley, *The Manchus*, Oxford, Blackwell, 1997.

Valerie Hansen, *The Open Empire: a history of China to 1600*, New York, Norton, 2000.

Zhang Hongxing, *The Qianlong Emperor: treasures from the Forbidden City*, Edinburgh, National Museums of Scotland, 2002.

Yu Zhuoyun and Graham Hutt, *Palaces of the Forbidden City*, Harmondsworth, Viking, 1984.

Reginald Johnston, *Twilight in the Forbidden City* [1934], Hong Kong, Oxford University Press, 1987.

Maggie Keswick, *The Chinese Garden*, London, Frances Lincoln, 2003.

Chang Kwang-chih (ed.), *Food in Chinese Culture: anthropological and historical perspectives*, New Haven, Yale University Press, 1977.

Der Ling, *Two Years in the Forbidden City*, London, Fisher and Unwin, 1912.

Ann Paludan, *The Imperial Ming Tombs*, London, Yale, 1981.

Evelyn S. Rawski, *The last Emperors: a social history of Qing imperial institutions*, Berkeley, University of California Press, 1998.

Jonathan Spence, *Emperor of China: self-portrait of K'ang-hsi*, London, Jonathan Cape, 1974.

Shih-shan Henry Tsai, *The Eunuchs in the Ming Dynasty*, New York, State University of New York Press, 1996.

Shih-shan Henry Tsai, *Perpetual Happiness: the Ming emperor Yongle*, Seattle, University of Washington Press, 2001.

Index

Picture credits